Table of content

LIST OF ABBREVIATIONS

ABSTRACT

INTRODUCTION

Context 8

Research Question 15

Methodology 16

Delimitation 18

Thesis Structure 21

HOW DO SOCIAL MEDIA REGULATE FREEDOM OF EXPRESSION?

Meta 26
    Facebook 27
    Instagram 30

The Oversight Board 34

Twitter 37

Sub-Conclusion 40

INTERNATIONAL LAW

What is the law? 43
    The International Covenant on Civil and Political Rights 43
    UN Guiding Principles 54

What is the application of the law 63
    The International Covenant on Civil and Political Rights 64
    UN Guiding Principles 84

Sub-Conclusion 100

REGIONAL LAW

What is the law? 104

What is the application of the law? 111

Sub-Conclusion 137

ASSESSMENT OF POLICY

Regional regulation 142
    Known regulation 142
    New initiatives 158

National regulation 165
    Germany 165
    The United Kingdom 167

Self-regulation 176

Sub-Conclusion 189

CONCLUSION

LITERATURE LIST

List of abbreviations

- **The United Nations**: UN
- **The Universal Declaration of Human Rights:** UDHR
- **The International Covenant on Civil and Political Rights**: ICCPR
- **The United Nations Guiding Principles on Business and Human Rights**: UNGPs
- **The European Convention on Human Rights**: ECHR
- **The European Court of Human Rights**: ECtHR
- **The European Union Charter of Fundamental Rights**: CFR
- **The European Union:** EU
- **The European Court of Justice**: CJEU
- **The United Nations Human Rights Council Resolution on the Promotion, Protection and Enjoyment of Freedom of Expression on the Internet:** RPFEI
- **Digital Service Act:** DSA
- **Network Enforcement Act:** NetzDG

- **Online Safety Bill:** The Bill

Abstract

Ensuring effective protection of the freedom of expression on social media platforms is increasingly important, as more and more of our lives are being lived online, especially on social media. This thesis explores how social media companies protect freedom of expression online, and if their measures cohere with the same protections arising under international- and regional human rights law.

This is done by exploring the scope of social media platforms' guidelines regarding the freedom of expression, and the scope and application of international- and regional human rights law. Then comparing if the measures social media platforms have adopted align with international- and regional regulations. Furthermore, it briefly delves into possible solutions to the problems found in the analysis.

It can be concluded that international-and regional human rights law leaves the direct regulation of social media platforms outside its reach. International- and regional institutions try to push States to regulate nationally, but this poses a problem with a decentralized system of regulation. The regional institution seeks to implement new regulation that aims to bind social media companies to protect the freedom of expression, and implement consequences when the companies do not comply. However, companies seem to have an interest in aligning with international- and regional human rights law, even if they are not legally bound by it. It is good that social media companies seem to align their measures with already existing legally binding human rights laws, but it is a precarious situation. As long as companies are left to self-regulate, their alignment with international and regional human rights law can change at any time. This creates a fragile foundation for the freedom of expression of the users of social media platforms.

Introduction

Context

Freedom of expression can be considered one of the principal fundamental human rights.[1] It is a right that applies in both the online and the offline sphere, and it is a right that has been protected in several international and national human rights regulations.[2]

The idea of the right to freedom of expression has been long-lasting. This idea can be seen in a letter by Donatien Alphonse François de Sade from 1793; *"Free communication of thoughts and opinions is one of man's most precious rights; every citizen can therefore speak, write, and publish freely…"*[3] This idea has been seen echoed in various legislations, both on a national and

---

[1] DigWatch, 'Freedom Of Expression Online In 2022 | DW Observatory' <https://dig.watch/topics/freedom-expression> accessed 25 June 2022.
[2] DigWatch (n 1).
[3] Nicholas Harrison, 'Freedom of Expression in History and in Theory', *Circles of Censorship* (University Press 1996) 9.

an international level, as can be seen in art. 19 of the Universal Declaration of Human Rights; *"Everyone has the right to freedom of opinion and expression; this right includes freedom to hold opinions without interference and to seek, receive and impart information and ideas through any media and regardless of frontiers."*[4] The right to freedom of expression is one of the human rights that have taken a continuous center stage as vitally important not only for the individual but also for the modern society and democracy itself. The right to freedom of expression has not become less relevant as the years have gone by. With the emergence of the internet, it has become an even more prevalent topic for lawmakers, companies, and ordinary users of the internet.

Since the birth of social media platforms, the online environment has drawn people in, with a promise of liberation in the form of empowerment to the user to; communicate, voice protest, scrutinize governments, and bring wrongdoings

---

[4] United Nations, 'Universal Declaration of Human Rights' (*United Nations*) Art. 19 <https://www.un.org/en/about-us/universal-declaration-of-human-rights> accessed 25 June 2022.

to light.⁵ In many ways the internet, and social media platforms especially, have become a modern-day soapbox, from where users can express their opinions about the things that are close to their hearts, and be heard by a broad audience from all across the globe. As a result, the presence of social media in the everyday lives of ordinary people has become immense, especially for the younger generation.⁶ In 2018, Facebook had an estimated 2.26 billion users, which means around 1 in 3 people in the world use Facebook.⁷ Facebook is, of course, only one of many social media platforms. In 2018, the ten biggest platforms had between 2.26 billion and 246.5 million active users on their respective platforms.⁸ This means that most large social media platforms have more active users than many countries have citizens.

---

⁵ Barrie Sander, 'Democratic Disruption in the Age of Social Media: Between Marketized and Structural Conceptions of Human Rights Law' (2021) 32 European Journal of International Law 159, 2.
⁶ Esteban Ortiz - Ospina, 'The Rise of Social Media' (*Our World in Data*) <https://ourworldindata.org/rise-of-social-media> accessed 15 August 2022.
⁷ Ortiz - Ospina (n 6).
⁸ Ortiz - Ospina (n 6).

The nature of social media platforms is that it has the potential for everyone to exercise their right to freedom of expression by voicing their opinions to a large and diverse group of users.[9] It is no secret that this potential is not going to waste; the social media platforms are currently being used by not only the ordinary people to voice their opinions but also by prominent figures from all around the world. This use of social media platforms is not, however, only being used for the common good and the furthering of prosperous democratic societies.[10]

In theory, social media should support an effective democratic process by enabling the individuals' right to freedom of expression. Instead, it seems as if this tool of liberation might gnaw at the very structure of democracy and human rights protection around the world.[11] The exercise of freedom of

---

[9] Rikke Frank Jørgensen and Lumi Zuleta, 'Private Governance of Freedom of Expression on Social Media Platforms: EU Content Regulation through the Lens of Human Rights Standards' (2020) 41 Nordicom review 51, 1.

[10] Jørgensen and Zuleta, 'Private Governance of Freedom of Expression on Social Media Platforms' (n 9) 1.

[11] Sander (n 5) 2.

expression on social media brings the dangers of harmful content being spread, just as widely, as any other type of content.[12] The harmful content also have the capability to spread much more widely than before, because of the inherent body and borderless nature of social media. Anything posted on social media, has the potential to spread to users across the world within seconds, and for some users, this can have a very damaging effect on their mental- and physical health.[13]

Freedom of expression is a large and complex area where the law provided by the public actors and the guidelines provided by the private actors leaves a large grey area to be explored. The online environment is increasingly being controlled by a

---

[12] Rikke Frank Jørgensen and Lumi Zuleta, 'Private Governance of Freedom of Expression on Social Media Platforms: EU Content Regulation through the Lens of Human Rights Standards' (2020) 41 Nordicom Review 51, 1.

[13] Karen and Feldscher, 'How Social Media's Toxic Content Sends Teens into "a Dangerous Spiral"' (*Harvard T.H Chan*, 8 October 2021) <https://www.hsph.harvard.edu/news/features/how-social-medias-toxic-content-sends-teens-into-a-dangerous-spiral/> accessed 16 August 2022.

small number of companies with platforms such as Facebook, Instagram, and Twitter.[14] These private companies have been able to control the content on their platforms largely without the interference of regulation from both national and international fronts. Now, policymakers are increasingly focusing on trying to get private actors to regulate the content on their platforms.[15] There is an ever-growing concern for the implications of private actors governing the online public sphere and the human rights implications thereof.[16] Social media platforms can be argued to be a new public space, owned by a private actor. This private actor is largely free to decide what guidelines to put in place.[17] Mark Zuckerberg, who is the CEO of Meta, which is the company behind Facebook, stated that; *"I understand people are concerned that*

---

[14] Sander (n 5) 2.

[15] Jørgensen and Zuleta, 'Private Governance of Freedom of Expression on Social Media Platforms' (n 9) 2.

[16] Jørgensen and Zuleta, 'Private Governance of Freedom of Expression on Social Media Platforms' (n 9) 2.

[17] Jørgensen and Zuleta, 'Private Governance of Freedom of Expression on Social Media Platforms' (n 9) 2.

we have so much control over how they communicate on our services."[18] Through this statement, it can be argued that the even the private actors such as Facebook, are aware of the complex climate that the right to freedom of expression has been put into.

The private actors behind platforms such as Facebook, Instagram, and Twitter, operate outside the direct reach of human rights law.[19] This is arguably worrisome because it places the right to freedom of expression in a vulnerable position outside the protective sphere of human rights law.[20] Dafna Dror-Shpoliansky and Yuval Shany write; *"The more cyberspace becomes a site where basic human rights are*

---

[18] Facebook, 'Mark Zuckerberg Stands for Voice and Free Expression' (*Meta*, 17 October 2019) <https://about.fb.com/news/2019/10/mark-zuckerberg-stands-for-voice-and-free-expression/> accessed 11 August 2022.

[19] Jørgensen and Zuleta, 'Private Governance of Freedom of Expression on Social Media Platforms' (n 9) 1.

[20] Jørgensen and Zuleta, 'Private Governance of Freedom of Expression on Social Media Platforms' (n 9) 2.

enjoyed or infringed, the greater is the expectation that public bodies charged with upholding human rights norms would take action to protect the rights of online users."[21] The eyes of the users of social media platforms are turned to, not only the private actors, but also the public actors for the protection their human rights.

Research Question

How do social media companies protect freedom of expression online, and do their measures cohere with the same protections arising under international and regional human rights law?

Methodology

This thesis makes use of the doctrinal method, which will be understood as exploring 'what is the law and private regulation,

---

[21] Dafna Dror-Shpoliansky and Yuval Shany, 'It's the End of the (Offline) World as We Know It: From Human Rights to Digital Human Rights – A Proposed Typology' (2021) 32 European Journal of International Law 1249, 3.

and how it has been applied'.²² This method will be used when analyzing legal sources and defining the scope of the law. In addition, it will be applied when analyzing how the law has been applied to the freedom of expression online and how this can be related to social media specifically.

Furthermore, throughout this thesis, there will be a focus on identifying problems and suggesting solutions to those problems while also focusing on the political and economic aspects of those solutions, which in other words, will lead to a discussion of politics. This will be done utilizing the New Haven Approach, which; *"[...]acts as a blueprint of social reality by applying the legal principles in the wider social context."*²³ The approach will help to; *"[...] understand the decision-making processes behind international policies and rules."*²⁴, and provide the tools for; *"[...] considering a large*

---

²² Suzanne Egan, 'The Doctrinal Approach in International Human Rights Scholarship' 2 <https://papers.ssrn.com/abstract=3082194> accessed 6 October 2022.

²³ Deplano Rossana and Tsagourias Nikolaos K, *Research Methods in International Law: A Handbook* (Edward Elgar Publishing 2021) 145.

variety of cultural and societal factors in creating a framework for understanding and developing effective legal responses to complex problems."[25]The doctrinal method is useful when analyzing the content of the law, and defining the scope of the law. However, it is less effective when seeking to hold the content and scope of the law up against political and economic interests and analyzing the policy prescriptions that might be created due to gray areas within the law. Therefore, the New Haven approach will be used when analyzing the context that the law exists in and the societal impact upon law and policies.

Throughout the thesis, a comparative method will be used on a limited scale by holding international human rights regulation up against regional human rights regulation.[26] Furthermore, the method will be used throughout the assignment to illustrate how private actors decide in the cases regarding freedom of expression on their platforms, and if their cause of action

---

[24] Deplano Rossana and Tsagourias Nikolaos K (n 23) 131.
[25] Deplano Rossana and Tsagourias Nikolaos K (n 23) 146.
[26] Edward J Eberle, 'The Methodology of Comparative Law' 23, 52.

differs vastly from what can be found in both human rights law, but also in case law.

Delimitation

Private actors

There are many examples of private actors who seek to create guidelines for freedom of expression within their sphere, but for the purpose of this thesis, the focus will remain on social media platforms. Furthermore, the focus will remain on the guidelines that social media platforms impose upon the users of their platforms and not on internal guidelines imposed on their employees.

There is a wide array of social media platforms, but due to limitations to this assignment, there will be focused on Facebook, Instagram, and Twitter. The reason behind this is that all of the platforms have the opportunity to make use of different forms of expression, such as visual-based content and written content. These three companies can also be considered the most prominent social media platforms. Due to the size of the platforms, they arguably have the biggest role and responsibility when it comes to protecting the right to freedom of expression on their platforms.

The platform Facebook and Instagram are owned by the parent company Meta, but they have their guidelines and will be explored separately. Therefore, throughout the thesis, the company Meta will only be mentioned in the cases where it encapsulates both platforms. In all other instances, the names of the platforms will be used instead.

Law

The thesis will explore how international- and regional institutions regulate freedom of expression and how they have applied the law in cases related to freedom of expression online. It will also be used when comparing examples of how social media platforms have handled freedom of expression on their platforms.

Due to the size of the thesis, and the borderless nature of social media platforms, it will not be possible to look into all regulations, both treaties, and soft law, related to freedom of expression. Regulation will therefore be limited to the following:

- **International level:**
    - ***International Covenant on Civil and Political Rights***: This instrument will be the primary instrument to explore how the United Nations regulates freedom of expression.
    - ***UN Guiding Principles on Business and Human Rights***: This instrument will be used to explore how soft law can be utilized in regulating freedom of expression for private actors. Other soft law instruments touch upon placing duties upon private actors when it comes to freedom of expression online, such as "*The World Summit on the Information Society's Declaration of Principles*", and

"*Charter of Human Rights and Principles for the Internet*", but due to the size of the thesis, the soft law instruments have been limited to the UN Guiding Principles on Business and Human Rights.

- **Regional level:**
  - *The European Human Rights Convention*: This instrument will be used to explore how freedom of expression has been regulated on a regional level.

Thesis Structure

The second chapter will explore how social media platforms regulate freedom of expression on their platforms.

The third chapter will analyze if the measures the social media platforms have implemented align with international human rights law. The chapter will start with answering the question of 'what is the law' by looking at the content and scope of the ICCPR and the UNGPs. Then the chapter will look at the application, where it will be explored 'who does the law apply to', in order to determine if social media companies are obligated to follow the regulation or if it is based on free will. Then the chapter will explore if the measures social media platforms have implemented align with the protections that arise under international human rights law.

The fourth chapter will analyze if the measures the social media platforms have implemented align with regional human rights law. The chapter will start with answering the question of 'what is the law' by looking at the content and scope of the ECHR. Then the chapter will look at the application, where it will be explored 'who does the law apply to', in order to determine if social media companies are obligated to follow the regulation or if it is based on free will. Then the chapter will explore if the measures social media platforms have implemented align with the protections that arise under international human rights law.

The fifth chapter will discuss the alternative option of regulating freedom of expression. Here there will be touched upon three possible solutions to the problems faced in chapters three and four. Solution number one is developing an instrument with a direct horizontal effect on the regional level. The second solution is developing national legislation to cover the gray zones left by international- and regional human rights legislation. The third solution is allowing social media companies to self-regulate. In this chapter positives and negatives behind the different solutions will be explored, with a perspective on political and economic considerations behind the solutions.

The sixth chapter will contain the concluding remarks, and summarize the findings of the thesis.

How do Social Media regulate freedom of expression?

Studies show that around 48 % of adults in the U.S get their news from social media, at least sometimes.[27] Furthermore, nearly a third of Americans regularly get their news on Facebook, which corresponds to 31% of the population.[28] This means a relatively high percentage of Americans get their news regularly on social media. When looking at how the distribution of individuals getting their news regularly on social media platforms is on different platforms, the numbers help to draw a clearer picture. For example, around 55% of American Twitter users get their news from the platform regularly.[29] These numbers are reflected on Facebook, where 47% of

---

[27] Mason Walker and Katerina Eva Matsa, 'News Consumption Across Social Media in 2021' (*Pew Research Center's Journalism Project*, 20 September 2021) <https://www.pewresearch.org/journalism/2021/09/20/news-consumption-across-social-media-in-2021/> accessed 24 August 2022.

[28] Walker and Matsa (n 27).

[29] Walker and Matsa (n 27).

American users get their news regularly from the platform. In contrast, only 27% of American Instagram users do the same.[30] This means that social media has a far-reaching grasp on individuals who use their platforms.

The large private companies that run social media platforms have their way of regulating the user-created content on their platform. It can be argued that these private companies regulate more forms of expression than any government does.[31] On Facebook, billions of pieces of content run through the platform every day, which is an astounding scale of content to regulate daily.[32] Hidden within the billions of pieces of content that can be considered harmless or even helpful, there can also be content that can be considered harmful or at least of dubious

---

[30] Walker and Matsa (n 27).

[31] Susan Benesch, 'But Facebook's Not a Country: How to Interpret Human Rights Law for Social Media Companies' (*Yale Journal on Regulation*) 86 <https://www.yalejreg.com/bulletin/but-facebooks-not-a-country-how-to-interpret-human-rights-law-for-social-media-companies/> accessed 23 August 2022.

[32] Benesch (n 31) 87.

nature.³³ Harmful content can have both direct and indirect effect on the users of the platform, and that means that social media platforms can have an interest in regulating this type of content in a myriad of ways. The dubious content is, however, more challenging to determine if it is supposed to be removed or stay on the platform, and in some cases removing the content would mean a restriction of the users' voices of. Therefore, it begs the question, how do social media platforms regulate their content?

Meta

Mark Zuckerberg, the founder, chairman, and CEO of Meta, recently stated that laws and regulations that are being formed around the world are increasingly trying to undermine the freedom of expression.³⁴ He argues that in order to protect the right to freedom of expression; *"[...]we should: 1) write policy that helps the values of voice and expression triumph around*

---

³³ Benesch (n 31) 87.

³⁴ Facebook, 'Mark Zuckerberg Stands for Voice and Free Expression' (n 18).

the world, 2) fend off the urge to define speech we don't like as dangerous, and 3) build new institutions so companies like Facebook aren't making so many important decisions about speech on our own."

Though Facebook and Instagram are owned by the same company, community standards can be found in different places. Therefore, there will be a separation of the guidelines for the two platforms, and then the shared mechanism of the Oversight Board will be explored last.

Facebook

The company 'Meta' which is the company behind Facebook and quite a few other platforms such as Instagram, states in their Community Standards that they aim to; *"[...] create a place for expression and give people a voice."*[35] They seek to create a space where individuals are openly able to discuss

---

[35] Facebook, 'Facebook Community Standards | Transparency Centre' <https://transparency.fb.com/en-gb/policies/community-standards/> accessed 11 August 2022.

subjects that are important to them, even though other individuals might find them objectionable.[36] Furthermore, they state that their commitment to expression is principal, but they also recognize that the Internet creates an environment where there is an increased opportunity for abuse, and therefore there must be limits to the freedom of expression.[37]

Those limits to expressions on the platforms are:

- **Authenticity;** which means the content must not misrepresent who they are or what they are doing.[38]
- **Safety;** which means content that can pose a risk of harm to the physical security of individuals.[39]

---

[36] Facebook, 'Facebook Community Standards | Transparency Centre' (n 35).

[37] Facebook, 'Facebook Community Standards | Transparency Centre' (n 35).

[38] Facebook, 'Facebook Community Standards | Transparency Centre' (n 35).

[39] Facebook, 'Facebook Community Standards | Transparency Centre' (n 35).

- **Privacy;** which means Facebook aims to protect personal privacy and information.
- **Dignity;** which means that individuals using the platform must respect the dignity of other individuals and are not to harass or degrade them.[40]

Therefore, the freedom of expression on the platform is not without limits, but those limits can be stretched to allow content that would not normally be allowed if it is 'newsworthy', and in the public interest.[41] Facebook will weigh the public interest in the content against the risk of harm.[42] In this case, Facebook actively referees to looking at international human rights standards to make the judgements.[43]

---

[40] Facebook, 'Facebook Community Standards | Transparency Centre' (n 35).

[41] Facebook, 'Facebook Community Standards | Transparency Centre' (n 35).

[42] Facebook, 'Facebook Community Standards | Transparency Centre' (n 35).

[43] Facebook, 'Facebook Community Standards | Transparency Centre' (n 35).

Instagram

Instagram's community guidelines start with the following sentence: *"We want Instagram to continue to be an authentic and a safe place for inspiration and expression. Help us foster this community. Only post your own photos and videos and always follow the law. Respect everyone on Instagram, don't spam people or post nudity."*[44] This does, in large, echo the outlines seen when looking at the guidelines on Facebook.

Some of the guidelines that Instagram has set up are more relevant to the freedom of expression than others. The headlines with the most relevance to the freedom of expression are:

- **Post photos and videos that are appropriate for a diverse audience**: There is also an emphasis on keeping the photos and videos on the platform

---

[44] Instragram, 'Community Guidelines | Instagram Help Centre' <https://help.instagram.com/477434105621119?cms_id=477434105621119&published_only=true> accessed 11 August 2022.

appropriate for a wide range of people.[45] This means that nudity is not allowed on the platform, just as seen on Facebook.

- **Follow the law**: Instagram explicitly outlines that users must follow the law.[46] Here, the guidelines state, specifically, that users must follow the law when posting on their platform. The content must, for example, not support terrorism, organized crime, or hate groups.[47] Furthermore, the platform does not allow for offering/selling sexual services, firearms, alcohol, tobacco between private persons, non-medical or pharmaceutical drugs.[48]

- **Respect other members of the Instagram community:** Instagram, much like Facebook, does not allow content that contains; *"[...] credible threats or hate speech, content that targets private individuals to degrade or shame them, personal*

---

[45] Instragram (n 44).
[46] Instragram (n 44).
[47] Instragram (n 44).
[48] Instragram (n 44).

*information meant to blackmail or harass someone, and repeated unwanted messages."*⁴⁹

- **Be thoughtful when posting newsworthy events:** Here, Instagram recognizes that the platform is being used to share newsworthy events, but the platform asks users to be careful when posting issues that can involve graphic images.⁵⁰

- **Help us keep the community strong:** Under this headline, the platforms ask if users see things that violate the guidelines that they report it.⁵¹

The consequence of breaching the guidelines may result in; "*[...] deleted content, disabled accounts or other restrictions.*" ⁵² Instagram states that just because a user finds content that is not to their liking, it does not mean that it violates their guidelines, and in such a case, the platform will not remove the

---

⁴⁹ Instragram (n 44).

⁵⁰ Instragram (n 44).

⁵¹ Instragram (n 44).

⁵² Instragram (n 44).

content, but instead, the user has the possibility of unfollowing or blocking the person who posted the content.[53]

Just as Facebook, Instagram referees to some instances where content that is generally considered to be against their guidelines may be allowed on the platform if it is; *"[...] newsworthy and in the public interest."*[54] Furthermore, they state, just as Facebook has done, this is only done after weighing the public interest value against the risk of harm and looks to international human rights standards to make the judgements.

The Oversight Board

Meta has created an institution called the Oversight Board. The Oversight Board aims to help Meta resolve what content to leave on their platform, what content to take down, and why.[55] The Board is established as an 'external body', where people

---

[53] Instragram (n 44).

[54] Instragram (n 44).

[55] Meta, 'The Oversight Board | Transparency Center' <https://transparency.fb.com/da-dk/oversight/> accessed 23 October 2022.

can appeal decisions made by Meta, can be appealed to.[56] Meta has stated that; *"We're committed to implementing the board's content decisions, and their recommendations help shape how we govern our policies."*[57]

If users of either Instagram or Facebook disagree with decisions the company has made regarding content on the platforms, they can appeal the decision to the Oversight Board.[58] Users can appeal the decision about;

- *"Most content that you posted on Facebook or Instagram that has been taken down".*[59]
- *"Most content posted by another person that has been left up on Facebook or Instagram."*[60]

---

[56] Meta, 'The Oversight Board | Transparency Center' (n 55).

[57] Meta, 'The Oversight Board | Transparency Center' (n 55).

[58] Meta, 'How to Appeal to the Oversight Board | Transparency Centre' <https://transparency.fb.com/en-gb/oversight/appealing-to-oversight-board/> accessed 23 October 2022.

[59] Meta, 'How to Appeal to the Oversight Board | Transparency Centre' (n 58).

[60] Meta, 'How to Appeal to the Oversight Board | Transparency Centre' (n

The content that can be considered eligible for review is; posts and statuses, photos, videos, comments, and shares.[61]

The Oversight Board quotes that; *"All case decisions of the Board reference international human rights standards when assessing Meta's actions in relation to content, including but not limited to the right to freedom of expression."*[62] This means that they look to international law, both hard law and soft law when making decisions. [63]

In order for a person to make use of the Oversight Board, one has to obtain a reference ID, which is done by having already

---

58).
[61] Meta, 'How to Appeal to the Oversight Board | Transparency Centre' (n 58).
[62] 'The Oversight Board: Operationalizing the UN Guiding Principles on Business and Human Rights' 6 <https://www.ohchr.org/sites/default/files/2022-03/Oversight-Board.pdf> accessed 23 October 2022.
[63] 'The Oversight Board: Operationalizing the UN Guiding Principles on Business and Human Rights' (n 62) 6.

exhausted Meta's appeals process and having received the final decision by Meta.[64]

It is important to note that it is the primary goal of the Oversight Board to act independently from Meta in order to act as a second remedy option for users. One can argue that the Oversight Board cannot be entirely independent of Meta, as the funding comes from the company. However, the same argument can be used when arguing if national courts are independent of the States they are funded by. Even though one can argue both for and against the Oversight Board's impartiality, Meta has managed to create an operational grievance mechanism, which in theory, acts independently from the company's actions.

Twitter

Within their guidelines to conduct on their platform, Twitter writes; *"Twitter's purpose is to serve the public conversation.*

---

[64] Meta, 'How to Appeal to the Oversight Board | Transparency Centre' (n 58).

Violence, harassment and other similar types of behavior discourage people from expressing themselves, and ultimately diminish the value of global public conversation. Our rules are to ensure all people can participate in the public conversation freely and safely."[65] This statement gives an excellent overview of the essence of their guidelines and reflects the idea of social media giving all individuals an opportunity to voice their opinions.

The headlines of the guidelines that are most relevant to the freedom of speech are as follows:

- **Safety:** Twitter does not allow; the threat of violence, threat or promotion of terrorism/violent extremism, child sexual exploitation, abuse/harassment, hateful conduct, maintaining an account if one is a perpetrator of violent attacks, suicide or self-harm, sensitive media, illegal or certain regulated goods or services.[66]

---

[65] Twitter, 'The Twitter Rules: Safety, Privacy, Authenticity, and More' <https://help.twitter.com/en/rules-and-policies/twitter-rules> accessed 22 August 2022.

- **Authenticity:** Twitter does not allow; Platform manipulation, civic integrity, misleading and deceptive identities, or synthetic and manipulated media.[67]

Just as seen in the guidelines for both Facebook and Instagram, Twitter states that in some cases, they will allow content that is generally against the rules in order to; *"[...] help ensure people have an opportunity to see every side of an issue, there may be the rare occasion when we allow controversial content or behavior which may otherwise violate our Rules to remain on our service because we believe there is a legitimate public interest in its availability. Each situation is evaluated on a case by case basis and ultimately decided upon by a cross-functional team."*[68]

---

[66] Twitter, 'The Twitter Rules' (n 65).

[67] Twitter, 'The Twitter Rules' (n 65).

[68] Twitter, 'Twitter's Enforcement Philosophy & Approach to Policy Development' <https://help.twitter.com/en/rules-and-policies/enforcement-philosophy> accessed 23 August 2022.

Similar to the other two platforms, Twitter states that some of the factors that help them when determining if the content is 'newsworthy and in the legitimate public interest', is to look at the public impact of the content, the source of the content, and the availability of coverage.[69]

Twitter states that when defending and respecting their users' rights, such as the right to freedom of expression; *"[...] while grounded in the United States Bill of Rights and the European Convention on Human Rights, it is informed by a number of additional sources including the members of our Trust and Safety Council, relationships with advocates and activists around the globe, and by works such as United Nations Principles on Business and Human Rights."*[70]

Sub-Conclusion

Overall, this chapter to illustrates, there are two central means of regulation that social media companies make use of.

---

[69] Twitter, 'The Twitter Rules' (n 65).
[70] Twitter, 'The Twitter Rules' (n 65).

The first method is content regulation by implementing community standards that apply to the users of the different platforms. Some content moderation will happen naturally by individuals adhering to community standards. The other part of the content regulation will happen by the company making a decision about either removing content or leaving content on the platform. All the platforms have themes central to their guidelines and very much akin to each other. For example, the headlines of authenticity and safety are especially relevant to the freedom of expression are though they might be angled slightly differently depending on the platform. This means that when posting content on the platforms, users are not allowed to post expressions that threaten the safety on the platforms, which means expressions that are threatening or incite violence, or any expressions akin to this, are not allowed on the platforms. Furthermore, users are not allowed to post content that is misleading, manipulated, or the like. These are the central types of restrictions, but there are exceptions, which are 'newsworthiness' and if the content is 'in the public interest.

The second method is the adjudication of the standards, an action taken by institutions such as the Oversight Board. The Oversight Board is meant to be an independent grievance mechanism that aims to test Meta's decisions to decide on legality. The Oversight Board will be explored further in the coming chapters, as the Board is a clear example of a private actor using international regulation to protect the right to freedom of expression.

Facebook, Instagram, and Twitter all express that they use legal regulation to support their decisions when removing, or when limiting the freedom of expression on their platforms. This begs the question: How does international- and regional law regulate the right to freedom of expression online? Does international- and regional human rights regulation apply to social media platforms? Furthermore, are international- and regional human rights regulations relevant for social media platforms?

This chapter explored, overarching, how social media companies regulate the freedom of expression on their platforms. The following two chapters it will explore, how these measures align with the protections arising under international- and regional human rights law.

International Law

This chapter will explore whether social media platforms' measures align with international law, specifically the ICCPR and the UNGPs.

What is the law?

The International Covenant on Civil and Political Rights

The International Bill of Human Rights lies at the core of the legal framework that supports the foundation of the work of the UN Human Rights and its mechanism.[71] The International Bill of Human Rights is made up of the Universal Declaration of Human Rights, the International Covenant on Civil and Political Rights, and its two optional protocols, and the International Covenant on Economic, Social and Cultural Rights.[72] This thesis will focus on the following articles, which will be analyzed further in the coming chapters:

---

[71] United Nations, 'OHCHR | Instruments & Mechanisms' (*OHCHR*) <https://www.ohchr.org/en/instruments-and-mechanisms> accessed 9 September 2022.

- Art. 19 of the International Covenant on Civil and Political Rights (ICCPR)[73]

When a State enters into a treaty, they have an obligation to ensure that all individuals within the State can enjoy the rights that have been set out in the treaties.[74] In other words, the States that are parties to a treaty are required to respect, protect, and fulfill human rights.[75] The States' obligation to respect means that they must refrain from interfering with the

---

[72] United Nations, 'OHCHR | International Human Rights Law' (*OHCHR*) <https://www.ohchr.org/en/instruments-and-mechanisms/international-human-rights-law> accessed 10 September 2022.

[73] United Nations, 'International Covenant on Civil and Political Rights' (*OHCHR*) <https://www.ohchr.org/en/instruments-mechanisms/instruments/international-covenant-civil-and-political-rights> accessed 17 August 2022.

[74] United Nations, 'Protect Human Rights' (*United Nations*) <https://www.un.org/en/our-work/protect-human-rights> accessed 5 September 2022.

[75] United Nations, 'The Foundation of International Human Rights Law' (*United Nations*) <https://www.un.org/en/about-us/udhr/foundation-of-international-human-rights-law> accessed 17 August 2022.

enjoyment of individuals' human rights, and the obligation to protect means that the State has to actively protect the individuals from experiencing human rights abuses.[76] Lastly, the duty to fulfill means that States must actively seek to facilitate the enjoyment of human rights within their sphere.[77]

When States decide to ratify international human rights treaties, they accept the obligation to adopt domestic measures and legislation that are compatible with the obligations that they are placed under by international law.[78] If the national legal proceedings are insufficient to address infringements upon an individual's fundamental rights, the framework on the international level will be able to help ensure that the standards set forth by the United Nations are respected, implemented, and enforced on a national level.[79]

---

[76] Nations, 'The Foundation of International Human Rights Law' (n 75).
[77] Nations, 'The Foundation of International Human Rights Law' (n 75).
[78] United Nations, 'OHCHR | International Human Rights Law' (n 72).
[79] United Nations, 'OHCHR | International Human Rights Law' (n 72).

The Universal Declaration of Human Rights (UDHR) is the cornerstone of international human rights and the predecessor to much of the human rights regulations that will be touched upon in this thesis.[80] The UDHR was proclaimed by the United Nations General Assembly in 1948, as a common standard of achievement when it comes to human rights, and it is generally considered to have paved the way for many human rights treaties both on an international-, regional-, and national level.[81] Though, the UDHR is considered to be a significant influence on other international-, regional-, and national human rights regulation, it is not a treaty, and has not been signed or ratified by States.[82] The UDHR is not legally binding and does not impose obligations upon States or private actors, but it is

---

[80] United Nations, 'Universal Declaration of Human Rights' (*United Nations*) <https://www.un.org/en/about-us/universal-declaration-of-human-rights> accessed 17 August 2022.

[81] Nations, 'Universal Declaration of Human Rights' (n 4).

[82] Dag Hammarskjöld Library, 'Research Guides: UN Human Rights Documentation: Universal Declaration of Human Rights' <https://research.un.org/en/docs/humanrights/undhr> accessed 17 August 2022.

generally considered to be the foundation of international human rights law.[83]

Different from the UDHR, the International Covenant on Civil and Political Rights places obligations upon States that have decided to ratify the Covenant (ICCPR).[84] Currently, there are 173 State Parties and 6 Signatories to the ICCPR.[85]

Art. 19(1-2) of the ICCPR states that; "*1. Everyone shall have the right to hold opinions without interference. 2. Everyone shall have the right to freedom of expression; this right shall include freedom to seek, receive and impart information and ideas of all kinds, regardless of frontiers, either orally, in writing or in print, in the form of art, or through any other media of his choice.*"[86] This means that art. 19 of the ICCPR

---

[83] Nations, 'The Foundation of International Human Rights Law' (n 75).

[84] United Nations, 'International Covenant on Civil and Political Rights' (n 73).

[85] United Nations, 'OHCHR Dashboard' <https://indicators.ohchr.org/> accessed 17 August 2022.

[86] United Nations, 'International Covenant on Civil and Political Rights' (n

protects the right to freedom of opinion, and the freedom of expression. This includes the right to; "*[...] seek, receive and impart information and ideas of all kinds regardless of frontiers.*"[87] The article protects the right to see and receive information, regardless of the medium.[88] The protection includes audio-visual, electronic, and internet related modes of expression.[89] This means that States must ensure an environment that enables freedom of expression, and protects the individual's right to exercise this right.[90]

Art. 19(2) of the ICCPR protects expression that might be considered 'deeply offensive', even though this type of

---

73).

[87] United Nations, 'United Nations: International Covenant on Civil and Political Rights, CCPR/C/GC/34' (1967) 61 American Journal of International Law 870, 3.

[88] Evelyn Aswad, 'The Future of Freedom of Expression Online' (2018) 17 Duke Law & Technology Review 26, 36.

[89] United Nations, 'United Nations' (n 87) 3.

[90] Jørgensen and Zuleta (n 11) 54.

expression might be restricted or limited by art. 19(3) and art. 20.[91]

There are limits to art. 19 of the ICCPR. The limits can be found in art. 19 (3)(a-b) of the ICCPR; " *The exercise of the rights provided for in paragraph 2 of this article carries with it special duties and responsibilities. It may therefore be subject to certain restrictions, but these shall only be such as are provided by law and are necessary: (a) For respect of the rights or reputations of others; (b) For the protection of national security or of public order (ordre public), or of public health or morals."*[92] With the relatively few exceptions, the ICCPR does not dictate directly what forms of expression should be limited.[93] It allows States to restrict expression if it can prove that it lives up to the three-part test that is held within art. 19(3).[94] This three-part test can be described as:

---

[91] United Nations, 'United Nations' (n 87) 3.
[92] United Nations, 'International Covenant on Civil and Political Rights' (n 73).
[93] Benesch (n 31) 90.
[94] Aswad (n 88) 36.

- **Legality:** The restriction must be provided by law.
- **Necessity:** The restriction must be the least intrusive means.
- **Legitimacy:** The restriction must seek to achieve one of the following public interests:
    - The respect for the rights of others
    - The protection of national security
    - The protection of public order
    - The protection of public health
    - The protection of public morals

Furthermore, any restriction placed on forms of expression protected within the ICCPR art. 19 has to be in line with the other provision included in the ICCPR.[95] This means a restriction to freedom of expression, even if it passes the three-part test, must also not constitute, as, an example, discrimination.

---

[95] Aswad (n 88) 36.

International human rights law is generally considered, in practice, to afford different degrees of protection depending on what kind of category expression falls within.[96] As an example, statements of a political nature are usually afforded higher protection than 'harmful speech'.[97]

Within the ICCPR, some articles explain what kinds of expressions States are allowed and encouraged to prohibit. Art. 20 of the ICCPR states that; *"1. Any propaganda for war shall be prohibited by law. 2. Any advocacy of national, racial or religious hatred that constitutes incitement to discrimination, hostility or violence shall be prohibited by law."*[98] Furthermore, art. 20(1) states that: *"1. Each State Party to the present Covenant undertakes to respect and to ensure to all individuals within its territory and subject to its jurisdiction the rights recognized in the present Covenant, without distinction of any kind, such as race, colour, sex, language, religion, political or*

---

[96] Sander (n 5) 168.

[97] Sander (n 5) 168.

[98] United Nations, 'International Covenant on Civil and Political Rights' (n 73).

*other opinion, national or social origin, property, birth or other status."*⁹⁹These are all examples of legitimate reasons to limit freedom of expression.¹⁰⁰

As previously mentioned, States and not private actors are held responsible for human rights abuses. States must ensure an environment that enables freedom of expression and protects the individual's right to exercise this right.¹⁰¹States must not only protect the public sphere but also the sphere of the private actors.¹⁰² Therefore, States do not only incur negative obligations, where States are obligated to not inflict human rights abuses themselves, but also positive obligations, where States must protect individuals against abuses caused by a third party.¹⁰³

---

⁹⁹ United Nations, 'International Covenant on Civil and Political Rights' (n 73).

¹⁰⁰ Rikke Jørgensen and Lumi Zuleta, 'Private Governance of Freedom of Expression on Social Media Platforms' (2020) 41 Nordicom Review 51, 54.

¹⁰¹ Jørgensen and Zuleta (n 11) 54.

¹⁰² Jørgensen and Zuleta, 'Private Governance of Freedom of Expression on Social Media Platforms' (n 9) 54.

¹⁰³ Jørgensen and Zuleta, 'Private Governance of Freedom of Expression on

When it comes to social media platforms that are owned by private companies, the individuals' ability to enjoy their right to freedom of expression depends on whether the States have imposed national regulation that applies to said companies.[104] Furthermore, it also relies on whether the companies themselves are interested in voluntarily participate, and undertake their human rights obligations.[105]

UN Guiding Principles

A substantial part of the normative standard, which has been formed through politics and other international practices, has taken the shape of non-binding instruments.[106] 'Soft law', though non-binding, can have a far-reaching impact on

---

Social Media Platforms' (n 9) 54.

[104] Jørgensen and Zuleta, 'Private Governance of Freedom of Expression on Social Media Platforms' (n 9) 55.

[105] Jørgensen and Zuleta, 'Private Governance of Freedom of Expression on Social Media Platforms' (n 9) 55.

[106] Lagoutte Stéphanie, Gammeltoft-Hansen Thomas, and Cerone John, *Tracing the Roles of Soft Law in Human Rights* (First edition, University Press 2017) 1.

international law. Both as a first step in a 'norm-making' process, but also providing rules and technical standards that might be required in order to interpret and implement the existing rules.[107] In some cases, it can be argued that soft law fills a void left by international legislation.[108]

There is no generally accepted definition of 'soft law', but it can arguably be defined as a; *"[...]commonly used by international lawyers and is generally understood to refer to certain categories of norms, and at least some of these norms are having an undeniable impact on the interpretation, application, and development of international human rights law."*[109] Though, there is no clear definition of the term, it remains widely used when it comes to international law and the international community in general.[110]

---

[107] Lagoutte Stéphanie, Gammeltoft-Hansen Thomas, and Cerone John (n 106) 1.

[108] Lagoutte Stéphanie, Gammeltoft-Hansen Thomas, and Cerone John (n 106) 1.

[109] Lagoutte Stéphanie, Gammeltoft-Hansen Thomas, and Cerone John (n 106) 15.

Within the international human rights sphere, soft law can generally be considered to fill two overarching functions, norm-filling and norm-creating.[111] When they act as norm-filling, they supplement areas where there are already legally binding standards. Soft law does not substitute hard law, but it can help when filling interpretative gaps; "[…] *soft law formulates and reformulates the hard law of human rights treaties in the application of this law to specific states and cases.*"[112] When soft law acts as norm-creating, it is where there is currently no international hard law.[113] It can be argued that soft law has paved the way for hard law, even though not all soft law necessarily merge into hard law.[114]

---

[110] Lagoutte Stéphanie, Gammeltoft-Hansen Thomas, and Cerone John (n 106) 3.

[111] Lagoutte Stéphanie, Gammeltoft-Hansen Thomas, and Cerone John (n 106) 7.

[112] Lagoutte Stéphanie, Gammeltoft-Hansen Thomas, and Cerone John (n 106) 7.

[113] Lagoutte Stéphanie, Gammeltoft-Hansen Thomas, and Cerone John (n 106) 7.

[114] Lagoutte Stéphanie, Gammeltoft-Hansen Thomas, and Cerone John (n 106) 7.

For the purpose of this thesis, soft law will be used when looking at the international level of human rights law. Furthermore, it will focus specifically on the following examples of international human rights soft law:

- UN Guiding Principles on Business and Human Rights (UNGPs)

The UNGPs focus on the protection of human rights within the sphere of companies, both online and offline. The UNGPs sets forth principles specific to States and companies. This instrument has been chosen because it seeks to influence how companies regulate freedom of expression within their sphere.

The idea of wanting to bind companies to uphold international human rights law is not a new notion.[115] Companies have always had problems protecting human rights when it comes at the cost of profit. Companies, such as Nike, have been accused of endangering their workers' health due to bad work environment, and Shell has been accused of endangering the

---

[115] Benesch (n 31) 92.

health and livelihood of the people in the Niger Delta in Nigeria.[116]

This interest in actively binding companies to human rights standards can be seen in the case of a set of binding corporate human rights norms, *'Norms on the Responsibilities of Transnational Corporations and Other Business Enterprises with Regard to Human Rights',* which was set forth by a Sub-Commission of the UN Commission on Human Rights who tried to win approval for the norms, but failed.[117] The set of norms signaled a departure from the prevailing practice of voluntary compliance, as the norms were meant to be non-voluntary.[118] It abandoned the State orientated role as the legal

---

[116] John Gerard Ruggie, 'The Social Construction of the UN Guiding Principles on Business & Human Rights' 7 <https://www.hks.harvard.edu/publications/social-construction-un-guiding-principles-business-human-rights> accessed 23 August 2022.

[117] Pini Pavel Miretski and Sascha-Dominik Bachmann, 'The UN "Norms on the Responsibility of Transnational Corporations and Other Business Enterprises with Regard to Human Rights": A Requiem' (2012) 17 Deakin Law Review 5, 5.

subject of international law[119], and imposed obligations directly onto companies instead of requiring States to implement legislation on the national level in order to regulate the actions of companies.[120]

Professor of law Upendra Baxi states, regarding the fact that obligations of States may not be directly transposed to apply to companies; *"[...] the automatic affixation of obligations under international law to non-state entities articulates, to use a rather obsolete phrase regime, not elements of lex lata but those of de lege ferenda, not the positive law, but the law in the making, or high on a wish list."*[121] In other words, the norms reflected what may have been a good vision of future law, but they did not represent the law as it currently exists.[122] Furthermore, Baxi states that; *"The Norms succeed*

---

[118] Miretski and Bachmann (n 117) 8.

[119] Miretski and Bachmann (n 117) 9.

[120] Miretski and Bachmann (n 117) 10.

[121] U Baxi, 'Market Fundamentalisms: Business Ethics at the Altar of Human Rights' (2005) 5 Human rights law review 1, 14.

[122] Miretski and Bachmann (n 117) 10.

impressively when read as animated by the politics of desire that furnish an ideal utopia. However, in the present opinion, the Norms err on the side, not of caution, but exuberance."[123] Eventually, the norms were rejected. It can be argued that without political commitment, it is not possible to draw up a treaty.[124] In this situation, the political landscape was not favorable toward changing or expanding the terms of who can be seen as legal subjects in international law. The failure to establish 'hard law' in order to bind corporations to international human rights standards has instead resulted in a set of guiding principles.

Some initiatives have been introduced that are meant to provide guidance to companies in order to ensure compliance with human rights. However, these are not considered legally binding for the companies they aim to regulate. One of the initiatives the UN introduced was the UN Guiding Principles

---

[123] Baxi (n 121) 14.

[124] Deva Surya and Bilchitz David, *Human Rights Obligations of Business: Beyond the Corporate Responsibility to Respect?* (University Press 2013) 160.

on Business and Human Rights (UNGPs), and follows the; *"Protect, Respect and Remedy Framework."*[125] The Framework underlines that, as seen in the ICCPR, States have a responsibility to protect everyone within their jurisdiction from having their human rights abused by companies, which can be achieved by implementing effective laws and regulations.[126] Furthermore, the Framework addresses the responsibilities that businesses have when it comes to human rights, which is to respect human rights.[127] The UN Framework also states that; *"Importantly, the UN Framework clarifies that the corporate responsibility to respect human rights exists independently of States' ability or willingness to fulfil their duty to protect human rights. No matter the context, States and businesses*

---

[125] 'The UN Guiding Principles on Business And Human Rights - An Introduction' 2 <https://www.ohchr.org/sites/default/files/Documents/Issues/Business/Intro_Guiding_PrinciplesBusinessHR.pdf> accessed 20 August 2022.

[126] 'The UN Guiding Principles on Business And Human Rights - An Introduction' (n 125) 2.

[127] 'The UN Guiding Principles on Business And Human Rights - An Introduction' (n 125) 2.

retain these distinct but complementary responsibilities."[128] In other words, by the standards of the UN Framework, businesses cannot hide behind the fact that States might not be upholding their responsibilities, thereby avoiding their responsibilities. Lastly, the UN Framework focuses on the facts that when the fundamental rights of an individual have been abused, there needs to be a system in place in order for the individual to gain an effective remedy.[129] For States, this effective remedy can be through a court-system or another non-judicial process, and for companies, it can be an effective grievance mechanism.[130]

According to the UNGPs, companies are required to respect, which in other words, means that they are required not to commit human rights abuses both directly and indirectly. The

---

[128] 'The UN Guiding Principles on Business And Human Rights - An Introduction' (n 125) 2.
[129] 'The UN Guiding Principles on Business And Human Rights - An Introduction' (n 125) 2.
[130] 'The UN Guiding Principles on Business And Human Rights - An Introduction' (n 125) 2.

expectations of the UN Guiding Principles on Business and Human Rights, specifically towards businesses, can be summed up as; policy commitment, human rights due diligence, and remedy mechanisms.[131]

What is the application of the law

When it comes to the application of the law in this specific case, it is of interest to look at two specific aspects. First, it is of interest to explore if the law can place obligations upon private actors directly, or the following the regulation would simply be a question of free will. This is interesting because it defines if adhering to the law can be seen as a choice or a matter of obligation for social media companies. Second, it is of interest to explore how international law and institutions have regulated freedom of expression in specific situations and how the social media companies' guidelines and decisions might compare to this.

---

[131] Jørgensen and Zuleta, 'Private Governance of Freedom of Expression on Social Media Platforms' (n 100) 55–56.

The International Covenant on Civil and Political Rights
Who does the law apply to?

The obligation to protect the right to freedom of expression is binding upon all Member States.[132] States are not only required to follow the obligations set forth in art. 19 of the ICCPR, it is also required to protect individuals from having their rights infringed upon by individuals or private actors.[133]

States are also required to ensure the protection contained within art. 19 of the ICCPR is implemented into the domestic law in a way that is aligned with the guidance that has been provided by the Committee.[134] It can also be argued that regulation should take into account the inherent difference between different forms of mediums for expression.[135] The Committee has stated that; "[…]*because of the development of modern mass media, effective measures are necessary to prevent such control of the media as would interfere with the*

---

[132] United Nations, 'United Nations' (n 87) 2.
[133] United Nations, 'United Nations' (n 87) 2.
[134] United Nations, 'United Nations' (n 87) 2.
[135] United Nations, 'United Nations' (n 87) 10.

right of everyone to freedom of expression."[136] This means that States should take steps towards ensuring that private companies do not gain too much control, in order; *"[...]to prevent undue media dominance or concentration by privately controlled media groups in monopolistic situations that may be harmful to a diversity of sources and views."*[137] Still, private media companies must not be set at a disadvantage compared to public media outlets.[138]

Internet companies, such as the companies behind social media platforms, have gained exceptional power to control individual's right to freedom of expression. It can be argued that these companies have had a positive role in furthering the ability to actively make use of the right to freedom of expression.[139] On the other hand, it can be argued that these

[136] United Nations, 'United Nations' (n 87) 10.
[137] United Nations, 'United Nations' (n 87) 10.
[138] United Nations, 'United Nations' (n 87) 10.
[139] United Nations, 'Promotion and Protection of All Human Rights, Civil, Political, Economic, Social and Cultural Rights, Including the Right to Development' 13 <https://primarysources.brillonline.com/browse/human-rights-documents-online/promotion-and-protection-of-all-human-rights-

private actors can become dangerous to the freedom of expression, either by accepting unlawful restriction imposed by States or by imposing restricting guidelines of their own.[140]

If States try to pressure companies into setting up a limitation to the freedom of expression, which might not live up to the three-part test, the companies might have a responsibility to defend the individual. This notion can be seen on Twitter's help center where they state: *"Defending and respecting the user's voice is one of our core values at Twitter."*[141] Twitter, furthermore, states that they challenge court orders to remove content, publish content removal demands, among other actions in order to actively defend their users' right to freedom of expression.[142] Responding to threats and demands made by

---

civil-political-economic-social-and-cultural-rights-including-the-right-to-development;hrdhrd99702016149> accessed 16 September 2022.

[140] United Nations, 'Promotion and Protection of All Human Rights, Civil, Political, Economic, Social and Cultural Rights, Including the Right to Development' (n 139) 13.

[141] Twitter, 'Twitter's Free Speech and Rights of People | Twitter Help' <https://help.twitter.com/en/rules-and-policies/defending-and-respecting-our-users-voice> accessed 23 August 2022.

States, is usually the way that private companies claim to use human rights regulation.[143]

It is, however, not unusual for companies to claim that they use international human rights law as a guideline when looking at cases. Twitter has cited using a myriad of well-known international human rights laws and guidelines when deciding on cases. [144] Facebook, or rather their Oversight Board, which independently reviews their decisions about content removal or banning, has also quoted using international human rights law as a standard. An example, is the case of the removal of former President Donald Trump from all of Meta's platforms; the Board analyzed the human rights responsibilities that Facebook might carry in this case by looking at international human

---

[142] Twitter, 'Twitter's Free Speech and Rights of People | Twitter Help' (n 141).

[143] 'United Nations, General Assembly, A/HRC/38/35' 5 <https://documents-dds-ny.un.org/doc/UNDOC/GEN/G18/096/72/PDF/G1809672.pdf?OpenElement> accessed 15 September 2022.

[144] Twitter, 'Twitter's Free Speech and Rights of People | Twitter Help' (n 141).

rights standards.¹⁴⁵ This suggests that even though Facebook might not be directly bound by international-or regional human rights standards, it still serves as a guideline. It is clear that the Oversight Board has been inspired by the tree-part test by looking at legality, legitimacy, necessity, and proportionality in the case.¹⁴⁶

In the UN Special Rapporteur Annual Rapport from 2018, it was recommended that a framework was implemented for the moderation of user-generated content that puts human rights at the center online.¹⁴⁷ Furthermore, there was a focus on companies needing to align their guidelines with art. 19(3) of the ICCPR, and the test of legality, necessity, and legitimacy.¹⁴⁸ The report states that; *"companies apply human rights*

---

[145] Oversight Board, 'Oversight Board | Independent Judgement. Transparency. Legitimacy - Decision FB-691QAMHJ' Case decision 2021-001-FB-FBR <https://www.oversightboard.com/decision/FB-691QAMHJ/> accessed 15 September 2022.

[146] Oversight Board, 'Oversight Board | Independent Judgement. Transparency. Legitimacy - Decision FB-691QAMHJ' (n 145).

[147] Aswad (n 88) 41.

[148] Aswad (n 88) 41.

principles in their operations, and most that do see them as limited to how they respond to government threats and demands."[149] The report focuses on the fact that aligning their guidelines with international human rights law would be in their best interest, as the guidelines would have their beginnings in universally agreed principles:[150]*"Rather than defending their "homegrown" versions of the appropriate parameters on worldwide speech, companies would be on firmer ground in discussions with governments (which often want them to censor too much speech) if their speech codes were aligned with international human rights protections."*[151]

Even though some companies may look to international human rights law when moving around in the realm of protection and limitation of human rights, it is not something that can be enforced by the United Nations. Therefore, States have an inherent interest in shaping the sphere that companies moderate their content within.[152] States have tried to do this by

---

[149] Aswad (n 88) 42.

[150] Aswad (n 88) 42.

[151] Aswad (n 88) 42.

implementing national legislation that places obligations upon private companies.[153] This does, however, mean that the actual regulation of the companies is left outside the direct sphere of international human rights law, and the regulation only affects the national regulation implicitly.

Overall, this means that the ICCPR does not directly bind companies; they can choose to look to international human rights when making decisions about content and guidelines on their platforms. They can also choose to look to other international human rights regulations, such as soft law, which will be discussed in the following.

How has the law been applied?

In the following, it will be explored if the measures the social media platforms have set forth, and the decisions they have made, align with international regulation.

---

[152] 'United Nations, General Assembly, A/HRC/38/35' (n 143) 6.
[153] 'United Nations, General Assembly, A/HRC/38/35' (n 143) 7.

The Special Rapporteur has stated that; *"[...] the Internet is one of the most powerful instruments of the 21st century for increasing transparency in the conduct of the powerful, access to information, and for facilitating active citizen participation in building democratic societies."*[154] The Special Rapporteur states that unlike other known types of media, such as radio, TV, or newspapers, the Internet holds the distinct difference in that it is a two-way medium that facilitates a participatory environment.[155] In the opinion of the Special Rapporteur the Internet has now become a key means for individuals to exercise the right enshrined in art. 19 of the ICCPR.[156] In the wording of art. 19 of the ICCPR, whereby any media can be

---

[154] United Nations, 'Promotion and Protection of All Human Rights, Civil, Political, Economic, Social and Cultural Rights, Including the Right to Development' (n 139) 4.

[155] United Nations, 'Promotion and Protection of All Human Rights, Civil, Political, Economic, Social and Cultural Rights, Including the Right to Development' (n 139) 6.

[156] United Nations, 'Promotion and Protection of All Human Rights, Civil, Political, Economic, Social and Cultural Rights, Including the Right to Development' (n 139) 7.

used to express oneself, it can be argued that the ICCPR has been drafted with the future development in technology in mind, which in turn means that the framework remains relevant and applicable today.[157]

When applying freedom of expression in the online sphere, one of the main instruments is the UN Human Rights Council Resolution on the promotion, protection, and enjoyment of freedom of expression on the Internet (RPFEI).[158] The RPFEI; *"Affirms that the same rights that people have offline must also be protected online, in particular freedom of expression, which is applicable regardless of frontiers and through any media of one's choice, in accordance with articles 19 of the Universal Declaration of Human Rights and the International Covenant on Civil and Political Rights;"[159]* In RPFEI there is a direct reference to the fact the right to freedom of expression, is

---

[157] United Nations, 'Promotion and Protection of All Human Rights, Civil, Political, Economic, Social and Cultural Rights, Including the Right to Development' (n 139) 7.

[158] DigWatch (n 1).

[159] 'United Nations, General Assembly, A/HRC/20/L.13'.

equally applicable in both the offline and the online sphere. This resolution does not in itself hold any powers of enforcement, but it can still be argued to be an important step in the right direction to upholding human rights on the internet.[160]

This means that the freedom of expression, protected by art. 19 of the ICCPR, cannot be limited to the offline world but it also applies the online world. It is clear that the United Nations finds International human rights law to apply to the internet, and social media companies seem to agree. Especially the Oversight Board regularly states in cases that their analysis of Meta's responsibilities regarding freedom of expression was informed by art. 19 of ICCPR.

Since institutions such as the Oversight Board and the social media platforms themselves have cited that they make use of international law, whereas some have directly cited art. 19 of the ICCPR, it is prudent to look at what limitations are

---

[160] Susan Park, 'The United Nations Human Rights Council's Resolution on Protection of Freedom of Expression on the Internet as a First Step in Protecting Human Rights Online' 32, 1130.

permitted under international law and how it compares to how social media platforms have currently regulated content.

There are many different ways that States might limit the freedom of expression online. Some of these are:

- **Arbitrary blocking or filtering of content**: Here, States block or filter content, which prevents users from seeing or accessing it.[161]
- **Criminalization of legitimate expression**: Here, States take action to limit the distribution of content by directly targeting the individual who seeks to receive or impart the information.[162]
- **Imposition of intermediary liability:** Here, States place liability upon the companies that act as intermediaries.[163]

---

[161] United Nations, 'Promotion and Protection of All Human Rights, Civil, Political, Economic, Social and Cultural Rights, Including the Right to Development' (n 139) 9.

[162] United Nations, 'Promotion and Protection of All Human Rights, Civil, Political, Economic, Social and Cultural Rights, Including the Right to Development' (n 139) 10.

As previously touched upon, not all forms of expression can necessarily be protected under art. 19(1-2). Art. 19(3) of the ICCPR lays out what type of expressions might be legitimately restricted, often with the aim to safeguard others and their human rights.[164] Such a limitation must live up to the three-part test of legality, legitimacy, necessity/proportionality, and such a restriction must also be applied by an independent body.[165] This means that a State must justify any limitations, and they must do so in the right way. This has been replicated by the Oversight Board when they analyze cases where the freedom of expression of art. 19 of the ICCPR can be considered to apply. This can be seen in the case of *Tigray Communication*

---

[163] United Nations, 'Promotion and Protection of All Human Rights, Civil, Political, Economic, Social and Cultural Rights, Including the Right to Development' (n 139) 11.

[164] United Nations, 'Promotion and Protection of All Human Rights, Civil, Political, Economic, Social and Cultural Rights, Including the Right to Development' (n 139) 8.

[165] United Nations, 'Promotion and Protection of All Human Rights, Civil, Political, Economic, Social and Cultural Rights, Including the Right to Development' (n 139) 8.

Affairs Bureau, where the Board upheld the decision made by Meta to remove a post that threatened violence in the conflict in Ethiopia.[166] In the case, the Board quotes the UN Special Rapporteur on freedom of expression; *"[...]companies do not have the obligations of Governments, their impact is of a sort that requires them to assess the same kind of questions about protecting their users' right to freedom of expression"*[167] Then they move on to analyzing;

- **Legality:** Where they found that the 'violence and incitement' policy was clear in terms of scope, but it was found that there was insufficient information on the implementation of the policy.[168]

---

[166] Oversight Board, 'Oversight Board | Independent Judgement. Transparency. Legitimacy. - Desicion 2022-006-FB-MR' <https://www.oversightboard.com/decision/FB-E1154YLY/> accessed 24 October 2022.

[167] Oversight Board, 'Oversight Board | Independent Judgement. Transparency. Legitimacy. - Desicion 2022-006-FB-MR' (n 166).

[168] Oversight Board, 'Oversight Board | Independent Judgement. Transparency. Legitimacy. - Desicion 2022-006-FB-MR' (n 166).

- **Legitimacy:** Where the Board found that the policy exists to prevent offline harm, which may be related to Facebook, and restrictions based on the policy serve the aim of protecting other fundamental rights.[169]
- **Necessity and proportionality**: Where the Board found that the removal of the content was necessary and proportionate limitation to the freedom of expression under international law.[170]

In this case, the Board found that it upheld that the limitation was justified. This structure is very reminiscent of the structure that the United Nations Human Rights Committee uses when examining cases. However, it is important to note that the three-part test is overarching and not limited to certain types of cases. One example of this is the case of *Mukong v. Cameroon*, where the applicant was arrested and detained after criticizing the Government and the President, and for meeting

---

[169] Oversight Board, 'Oversight Board | Independent Judgement. Transparency. Legitimacy. - Desicion 2022-006-FB-MR' (n 166).

[170] Oversight Board, 'Oversight Board | Independent Judgement. Transparency. Legitimacy. - Desicion 2022-006-FB-MR' (n 166).

to discuss the possibility of introducing a multi-party democracy.[171] In this case, the Committee stated that when examining the case based on the criteria found in the three-part test; *"[...] the HRC found that an unsubstantiated need to safeguard an alleged vulnerable state of national unity could not justify subjecting individuals to arrest, detention and inhuman treatment."*[172] This relates to the lack of legitimate aim of the limitation the State has made. Furthermore, the Committee stated that; *"[...] protecting and strengthening national unity cannot be achieved by muzzling advocacy for multi-party democracy and human rights."*[173]This statement, arguably, relates to the lack of necessity and proportionality of the limitation the State has implemented.

When the Oversight Board makes use of art. 19 of the ICCPR, the structure and measures they decide upon are very

---

[171] UNHRC, 'Mukong v. Cameroon' (*Global Freedom of Expression*) <https://globalfreedomofexpression.columbia.edu/cases/mukong-v-cameroon/> accessed 16 September 2022.

[172] UNHRC (n 171).

[173] UNHRC (n 171).

reminiscent of the way the United Nations Human Rights Committee handles cases regarding the right to freedom of expression art. 19 of the ICCPR. Though there are some twists to the way the test is applied, such as the legality test, where the Committee looks at actual regulation and the Board looks at policy, it still helps to support the Oversight Boards position as a legitimate grievance mechanism akin to a court-system.

Restrictions are not only negative. Limitations to the freedom of expression are necessary, and it can also be criticized if everyone is allowed to utter anything, especially if this ends up violating the rights of others. One way of describing speech that can fall within the scope of expression that should be limited is 'hate speech'. Hate speech has become much more prevalent with the rise of the internet, especially social media platforms. The term 'hate speech' is currently not clearly defined by international human rights law, but: *"[...] the United Nations Strategy and Plan of Action on Hate Speech defines hate speech as…"any kind of communication in speech, writing or behaviour, that attacks or uses pejorative or discriminatory language with reference to a person or a group on the basis of who they are, in other words, based on their religion, ethnicity, nationality, race, colour, descent, gender or other identity factor.*"[174] When it comes to limiting the freedom of expression, there is very much the aspect of balancing the right to freedom of expression against other rights, and principles such as equality, non-discrimination, and so on.[175]

The United Nations Secretary-General António Guterres, stated; "*Addressing hate speech does not mean limiting or prohibiting freedom of speech. It means keeping hate speech from escalating into something more dangerous, particularly incitement to discrimination, hostility and violence, which is*

---

[174] United Nations, 'What Is Hate Speech?' (*United Nations*) <https://www.un.org/en/hate-speech/understanding-hate-speech/what-is-hate-speech?gclid=EAIaIQobChMIus6h2ruW-gIVh6jVCh0QzANSEAAYASAAEgINtfD_BwE> accessed 16 September 2022.

[175] United Nations, 'International Human Rights Law -UN Actions against Hate Speech' (*United Nations*) <https://www.un.org/en/hate-speech/united-nations-and-hate-speech/international-human-rights-law> accessed 17 September 2022.

prohibited under international law."[176] The United Nations has made a link between hate speech and disinformation as the catalyst to human rights atrocities.[177] This notion that hate speech can amount to something that can potentially be dangerous for life and limb, can be seen in the case of **Faurisson v. France**. In the case **of Faurisson v. France,** the United Nations Human Rights Committee held that statements made by Faurisson, who doubted the existence and use of gas chambers during World War II, amounted to hate speech.[178] The Committee found that; *"Since the statements made by the author, read in their full context, were of a nature as to raise or strengthen anti-semitic feelings, the restriction served the*

---

[176] United Nations, 'Hate Speech versus Freedom of Speech' (*United Nations*) <https://www.un.org/en/hate-speech/understanding-hate-speech/hate-speech-versus-freedom-of-speech> accessed 16 September 2022.

[177] United Nations, 'Hate Speech and Real Harm' (*United Nations*) <https://www.un.org/en/hate-speech/understanding-hate-speech/hate-speech-and-real-harm> accessed 16 September 2022.

[178] UNHRC, 'Faurisson v. France' (*Global Freedom of Expression*) <https://globalfreedomofexpression.columbia.edu/cases/faurisson-v-france/> accessed 16 September 2022.

respect of the Jewish community to live free from fear of an atmosphere of anti-semitism."[179] This case illustrates the situation where a statement can constitute hate speech due the fact that it incites to discrimination and hostility. The fact that the expression is unpopular is not enough in itself. This cause of action can also be seen to be taken by social media platforms when they make decisions in cases about the removal of content.

In the case of **Knin Carton**, made by Meta's Oversight Board, the decision to leave posts on the platform depicting ethnic Serbs as rats was overturned by the Board.[180] The Board stated that removing the content would be consistent with the human rights responsibilities that Meta has as a business, by committing itself to follow various international guidelines and legislation.[181] When the Board looked at the three-part test

---

[179] UNHRC (n 178).
[180] Oversight Board, 'Oversight Board | Independent Judgement. Transparency. Legitimacy.- FB-JRQ1XP2M' <https://www.oversightboard.com/decision/FB-JRQ1XP2M/> accessed 17 September 2022.

found in ICCPR art. 19(3), especially under necessity and proportionality, stated; *"The content in this case, comparing ethnic Serbs to rats and celebrating past acts of discriminatory treatment, is dehumanizing and hateful. The Board would have come to a similar conclusion about any content that targets an ethnic group in this way, especially in a region that has a recent history of ethnic conflict. The Board finds removing this content from the platform was necessary to address the serious harms hate speech on the basis of ethnicity poses."*[182] This is very much in line with the UN regulation, where the protection of especially minorities and their enjoyment of human rights are front and center. Any limitations to the freedom of expression, such as those prescribed by art. 19(3) and art. 20(1-2) of the ICCPR must be carefully weighed and measured by States, but also by any private actors who might wish to make use of the regulation.

---

[181] Oversight Board, 'Oversight Board | Independent Judgement. Transparency. Legitimacy.- FB-JRQ1XP2M' (n 180).

[182] Oversight Board, 'Oversight Board | Independent Judgement. Transparency. Legitimacy.- FB-JRQ1XP2M' (n 180).

UN Guiding Principles

Who do the principles apply to?

The UN Guiding Principles on Business and Human Rights; *"[...] restate and compile relevant human rights obligations and create soft law standards addressing both states and business enterprises."*[183] It can be argued that in this way, the UNGPs can be considered to interact with both hard and soft law.[184] As previously touched upon, the UNGPs bring to light the private actors as the ones who carry the responsibility, a standard endorsed by the Human Rights Council, but it also touches upon the obligations of States outlined in hard law.[185]

---

[183] Lagoutte Stéphanie, Gammeltoft-Hansen Thomas, and Cerone John (n 106) 236.

[184] Lagoutte Stéphanie, Gammeltoft-Hansen Thomas, and Cerone John (n 106) 236.

[185] Thomas Gammeltoft-Hansen and others (eds), 'Introduction: Tracing the Roles of Soft Law in Human Rights', *Tracing the Roles of Soft Law in Human Rights* (Oxford University Press 2016) 236 <https://doi.org/10.1093/acprof:oso/9780198791409.003.0001> accessed 11 September 2022.

As mentioned earlier, the UN Guiding Principles on Business and Human Rights are non-binding, which means there is a reliance on the willingness of the companies to cooperate and adhere to the Framework. There is no element of 'force' as seen with laws implemented with the possibility of judicial consequence if it is not followed. On the other hand, as Jørgensen and Zuleta state, while quoting Kaye, the former UN Special Rapporteur on Promotion and Protection of the Right to Freedom of Opinion and Expression; *"While the Guiding Principles are nonbinding, the overwhelming role of social media companies in public life globally provides a strong argument for their adoption and implementation."* [186] The United States Government is among the countries that have encouraged companies to implement the guidelines and to treat said guidelines as a minimum standard rather than an unachievable one.[187]

---

[186] Jørgensen and Zuleta, 'Private Governance of Freedom of Expression on Social Media Platforms' (n 9) 55.

[187] Aswad (n 88) 38.

Even though the UNGPs are not legally binding, this does not stop social media platforms from referencing the guidelines in their community standards. For example, Twitter states that protecting their users' voices is a global commitment which is, among other sources, informed by the UNGPs.[188] Furthermore, the Oversight Board has contributed input to the practical application of the UNGPs to the UN High Commissioner for Human Rights.[189] Here they state that: *"In its corporate human rights policy, Meta affirmed that the Board was conceptualized in line with the effectiveness criteria of operational grievance mechanisms and access to remedy under the UN Guiding Principles on Business and Human Rights."*[190] This suggests that Meta has an interest in keeping in line with the Framework that the UNGPs propose. The fact that Meta actively establishes a grievance mechanism in order to live up to the

---

[188] Twitter, 'Twitter's Free Speech and Rights of People | Twitter Help' (n 141).

[189] 'The Oversight Board: Operationalizing the UN Guiding Principles on Business and Human Rights' (n 62) 2.

[190] 'The Oversight Board: Operationalizing the UN Guiding Principles on Business and Human Rights' (n 62) 3.

criteria of an effective remedy under the UNGPs suggest that though the guidelines are not legally binding, social media companies are not against aligning with them.

At first glance, it might seem like human rights law has been expanded by the UNGPs, because the instrument places obligations upon the private actors, but in reality, the scope of the legal protection has not been widened.[191] Lagoutte et al. argue that: *"[...] a discrepancy may occur between, on the one hand, civil society views (and discourse) on the emergence of new obligations for states and private actors and, on the other hand, the very clear opinion emanating from states that only international treaties and customs create international obligations."*[192] It can be argued that the implementation of the UNGPs can create some confusion as to who is obligated by international law directly, and which instruments have the power to impose international obligations.

---

[191] Lagoutte Stéphanie, Gammeltoft-Hansen Thomas, and Cerone John (n 106) 236.

[192] Lagoutte Stéphanie, Gammeltoft-Hansen Thomas, and Cerone John (n 106) 236.

The UNGPs both mention States and private actors. In the UNGPs, the States' duty to protect draws focus upon the positive obligation of the State to safeguard individuals against human rights abuses caused by private actors.[193] In practice, this means that it is the obligation of the State to ensure that companies do not indirectly abuse human rights of individuals.[194] If a case arises where a State is not protecting individuals against infringements, it can be argued that another State or even company might be responsible to take action.[195]

One thing is what the UNGPs seek to achieve and what it achieves in reality. There is plenty who critiques the UNGPs, for various reasons. First of all, it is important to note that the UNGPs are not aimed towards a specific sector but broadly address all companies.[196] This can result in some difficulty in

[193] Lagoutte Stéphanie, Gammeltoft-Hansen Thomas, and Cerone John (n 106) 238.

[194] Lagoutte Stéphanie, Gammeltoft-Hansen Thomas, and Cerone John (n 106) 238.

[195] Lagoutte Stéphanie, Gammeltoft-Hansen Thomas, and Cerone John (n 106) 238.

[196] Andreas Rasche and Sandra Waddock, 'The UN Guiding Principles on

applying the very generic framework that the UNGPs present.[197] On the one hand, it can be argued that companies have many similarities. Secondly, it can be argued that the human rights that can be violated may differ vastly from company to company, depending on their realm of business. When focusing on social media companies, human rights can be violated when the companies deal with their employees, but also when individuals access and use their platform and exercise various rights, such as the right to freedom of expression. Some scholars argue that the UNGPs should provide stricter guidelines with a higher level of detail, which in turn would result in less of an interpretation assignment for the companies, and it might help the application of the UNGPs in practice immensely.[198] It can be argued that this was not the intention of the UNGPs, but instead the aim of the first attempt to create legally binding norms in the area. Instead, the aim of the

---

Business and Human Rights: Implications for Corporate Social Responsibility Research' (2021) 6 Business and Human Rights Journal 227, 234.

[197] Rasche and Waddock (n 196) 234.

[198] Rasche and Waddock (n 196) 234.

UNGPs is to; *"[...]organize a difficult and contested discourse around three key pillars; they try to reduce conceptual confusion and promote consensus."*[199]

Justine Nolan argues that; *"Formulating and adopting coherent policies and gathering them into an international soft instrument is a positive step, but not sufficient."*[200] This stance argues that though the UNGPs are palatable for both States and companies; this aim to be palatable means that the UNGPs suffers the consequence of being unambitious when it comes to regulating companies, and protecting human rights such as the freedom of expression online.[201] The UNGPs run the risk of seeming as if it gives immense leeway to companies, where international law arguably sets a much stricter tone for States. This can result in, as M. K. Addo wrote well before the UNGPs were implemented; *"[...]only a selected few among private corporations are likely to willingly submit to new responsibilities without being legally compelled to do so."*[202]

---

[199] Rasche and Waddock (n 196) 235.
[200] Deva Surya and Bilchitz David (n 124) 160.
[201] Deva Surya and Bilchitz David (n 124) 160.

Today, at least on an international level, the notion of the duty of companies to protect human rights has remained as soft law instruments. This means that on an international level, participation in the protection of human rights is still largely voluntary for companies. Without hardening the instruments that apply to companies, one cannot expect the companies to actively seek to adhere to them unless it also has an economic benefit on their side. Therefore, the debate on the legal obligations and accountabilities of companies is still ongoing.[203]

How have the principles been applied?

If social media companies aim to live up to the UNGPs, apply them to their platforms, and subsequently respect the right to freedom of expression, they need to:

- Understand the scope of freedom of expression under international human rights law. [204]

---

[202] Deva Surya and Bilchitz David (n 124) 161.

[203] Deva Surya and Bilchitz David (n 124) 77.

[204] Aswad (n 88) 38.

- Asses the risk of infringement of human rights on their platforms. Asward states that the infringements frequently happen; " *[...]: (1) by cooperating with governmental demands that do not meet international human rights law standards (e.g., governmental demands to remove speech critical of the head of state) and (2) by imposing their own corporate speech codes on user-generated content that restrict speech otherwise protected under international human rights law.*"[205]

One way to tackle the first instance Asward referees to, is by questioning government demands and not complying with them blindly. The Global Network Initiative seeks, among other things, to help companies that have joined the network to challenge governmental demands that do not meet the standards of international human rights law.[206] Companies that have joined the network are expected to know and understand the scope of freedom of expression within international law,

---

[205] Aswad (n 88) 39.
[206] Aswad (n 88) 40.

and to be able to assess whether a demand made by the government, conforms with art. 19 of the ICCPR.[207] If the demand does not meet the standard of art. 19 of the ICCPR, the companies are expected to resist the demand of the government while still complying with local law.[208] An example of this principle can be found on Twitter's help center, where they explain; *"Some examples of steps we take to defend and respect our users include: [...]Challenges to court orders to remove content from our platform or disclose user data;[...]"*[209] This means that to some degree, the companies behind social media platforms have sought to challenge States, at least on a case-to-case basis. Another way companies can challenge government demands, is to refuse to offer their services in countries that implement restrictions that do not live up to international human rights law. For example, Mark Zuckerberg has stated that China's censorship of freedom of expression is a reason they refuse to offer any of their services in the country.[210] One

---

[207] Aswad (n 88) 40.

[208] Aswad (n 88) 40.

[209] Twitter, 'Twitter's Free Speech and Rights of People | Twitter Help' (n 141).

can argue that China would not allow Meta to operate in the country, and it is therefore not a choice the company has made. On the other hand, if Meta were easily bought, they might have traded the protection for profit immediately.

When it comes to the second instance, Asward referees to, it is worth considering if forcing companies to align with such guidelines might violate their right to freedom of expression.[211] Generally, companies are not considered to be protected under art. 19 of the ICCPR, due to companies are not considered to be protected under the term 'individuals'.[212] Therefore, if the UNGPs were legally binding, it would not violate the freedom of expression to require them to comply.[213] However, as Award states; *"If an American platform chooses not to respect international human rights in the content and enforcement of its speech code, it would not necessarily violate international*

---

[210] Facebook, 'Mark Zuckerberg Stands for Voice and Free Expression' (n 18).

[211] Aswad (n 88) 40.

[212] Aswad (n 88) 40.

[213] Aswad (n 88) 41.

or U.S. law, but it would be acting inconsistently with the global expectations embodied in the UNGPs."[214] State imposed censorship is well known, and is often relatively easy to spot as an individual; an example could be China blocking platforms that will not comply with their censorship.[215] Company imposed censorships can arguably be less transparent, an example thereof is;" *Facebook prohibits "hate speech" which certainly accords with international human rights law. However, in mid-2017, it was reported that the relevant Facebook algorithm seemed to be overly vigorous in protecting speech aimed against white men, and rather less effective in protecting Muslims. If true, Facebook's ban on hate speech does not yet seem to be implemented in a way that properly defines "hate speech"."*[216] On the one hand, it can be argued that this is indeed a way for the companies to fill their duty under the UNGPs to respect human rights. However, it can also

---

[214] Aswad (n 88) 41.

[215] Sarah Joseph, 'The Human Rights Responsibilities of Media and Social Media Businesses' 13 <https://papers.ssrn.com/abstract=3146730> accessed 30 September 2022.

[216] Joseph (n 215) 14.

be argued that such use of algorithms constitutes a violation of the right to freedom of expression.

The UNGPs focus on the concept of effective remedies, which applies to States and companies.[217] For companies, this means that when they identify their implication in a case of human rights abuse they should take steps to investigate the abuse, and provide remedy through a legitimate process.[218] The UNGPs' concept of remedies does not only touch upon what may be considered the standard methods of remedies, but also; *"[...]remedy may include apologies, restitution, rehabilitation, financial or non-financial compensation and punitive sanctions (whether criminal or administrative, such as fines), as well as the prevention of harm through, for example, injunctions or guarantees of non-repetition."*[219] There can be remedy mechanisms that are based in State-systems, but there are remedy mechanisms that can be based in the private actors' systems.

---

[217] Deva Surya and Bilchitz David (n 124) 331.
[218] Deva Surya and Bilchitz David (n 124) 331.
[219] Deva Surya and Bilchitz David (n 124) 331.

An example is the Oversight Board, and internal grievance mechanisms within Facebook, Instagram, and Twitter. The 'Protect, Respect and Remedy' Framework places remedies in the last pillar, which illustrates that when the States have failed to protect, and the companies have failed to respect, there must be a remedy as a natural response.[220] It can be argued that; *"Social media platforms, especially the largest ones like Facebook and Twitter that have enormous resources, should develop mechanisms to deal swiftly with complaints about content, and to facilitate the takedown of content that harms the human rights of others. Nevertheless, while algorithms can monitor and delete offending content, that logistical task is unfeasible within short enough timelines to prevent occasional serious harm to human rights."*[221] This suggests that not only traditional remedy mechanisms can be of use but also algorithms can be used as a form of remedy, as well as protecting against human rights abuses. The Oversight Board is an example of Meta seeking to live up to the UNGPs

---

[220] Deva Surya and Bilchitz David (n 124) 333.
[221] Joseph (n 215) 12.

effectiveness criteria by seeking to implement a grievance mechanism and access to remedy that exists 'separate' from Meta.[222]

It is important to note that, different from the ICCPR, the UNGPs do not seek to regulate what the ICCPR already regulates. In other words, the UNGPs do not set up guidelines on how to handle certain forms of expression, as can be seen with the ICCPR. Instead, the UNGPs focuses on the responsibility of the company to create the right framework, in order to respect already existing rights; *"The responsibility of business enterprises to respect human rights refers to internationally recognized human rights – understood, at a minimum, as those expressed in the International Bill of Human Rights [...]"*[223] In theory, this means that companies

---

[222] 'The Oversight Board: Operationalizing the UN Guiding Principles on Business and Human Rights' (n 62) 2.

[223] 'Guiding Principles on Business and Human Rights - Implementing the United Nations "Protect, Respect and Remedy" Framework' 18 <https://www.ohchr.org/sites/default/files/documents/publications/guidingprinciplesbusinesshr_en.pdf> accessed 12 September 2022.

can only adhere to the UNGPs by also adhering to, for example, the ICCPR. Companies cannot claim to follow the UNGPs, if they subsequently impose limitations that would not be allowed under the ICCPR. Therefore, if Meta implemented the Oversight Board based on the suggestions made by the UNGPs but did not measure their decisions against international human rights law, they would not live up to the UNGPs.

Sub-Conclusion

It can be concluded that art. 19 of the ICCPR protects the right to freedom of expression, both in an online and offline environment. Any limitations to art. 19 of the ICCPR have to live up to the three-part test, whereby a limitation must be legal, legitimate, and necessary/proportionate in order for it to be allowed under the ICCPR. The ICCPR is legally binding for States but not for private actors, therein social media companies. The only way the United Nations would be able to regulate social media companies would be to push States to regulate nationally. This means that social media companies choose to adhere to and align with the ICCPR. This can be considered problematic because this leaves the protection of the freedom of expression outside the direct reach of international human rights law and legal institutions. Even though social media companies are not bound to adhere to the ICCPR, much suggests that they do indeed seek to comply with the legislation. This can be seen when examining cases by the Oversight Board, where it has been found that they are using the three-part test when addressing limitations generally and in the form of hate speech, which follows by the ICCPR art. 19 and also by jurisprudence.

It can be concluded that the UNGPs seek to create a framework that actively addresses the companies' roles in respecting human rights, and ensuring an effective remedy when they fail to do so. Though it was the aim to begin with, the UNGPs are not legally binding for companies. Initially, the United Nations sought to bind companies to similar standards that States have to adhere to, but due to the lack of political support, this had to be abandoned. Therefore, it is based on the free will of the companies to follow the guidelines that have been set forth.

Even though the UNGPs are not legally binding, both Meta and Twitter have acknowledged the influence of the UNGPs on their guidelines and institutions. Meta has affirmed that the Oversight Board is the result of an interest in adhering to the UNGPs criteria of an effective remedy, which must be considered no small effort by the company.

Overall, it can be concluded that social media companies have the intention to follow the ICCPR and implement the framework found in the UNGPs. The implementation is not always successful, as can be seen with some cases brought before the Oversight Board, where the Board sometimes finds that Meta is not in compliance with its human rights responsibilities. This means that though the companies might seek to do their best to act in compliance and set up measures that cohere with international human rights law, it is not always the case. However, social media companies do show a willingness to comply with both the UNGPs and the ICCPR by actively trying to implement institutions and measures that align with the legislation.

The following chapter will build upon these conclusions by exploring if the measures that social media companies have implemented cohere with the protections found under regional human rights law.

Regional Law

This chapter will explore if the measures set forth by social media platforms align with regional human rights law, specifically, the ECHR.

What is the law?

The ECHR, much like the ICCPR, imposes obligations upon States that are parties to the Convention.[224] Currently, there are 47 State Parties, and these include the Member States of the Council of Europe, and the EU.[225] The European Court of Human Rights can decide complaints, which can be submitted by private actors or States concerning violations of the ECHR, committed by States.[226]

---

[224] International Justice Resource Center, 'European Court of Human Rights' (*International Justice Resource Center*, 10 July 2014) <https://ijrcenter.org/european-court-of-human-rights/> accessed 17 August 2022.

[225] International Justice Resource Center (n 224).

[226] International Justice Resource Center (n 224).

Art. 10 of the ECHR states that; *"Everyone has the right to freedom of expression. This right shall include freedom to hold opinions and to receive and impart information and ideas without interference by public authority and regardless of frontiers. This Article shall not prevent States from requiring the licensing of broadcasting, television or cinema enterprises."*[227] The ECtHR has, in the case of **Handyside v. The United Kingdom,** recognized that freedom of expression acts as one of the cornerstones in a democratic society, and it is one of the basic conditions for the progress of the society and for the development of the individuals within that society.[228] The Court has emphasized in both **Handyside v. the United Kingdom** and **Observer and Guardian v. United Kingdom** that art. 10 of the ECHR is not only applicable to information or ideas, which can be considered favorable, inoffensive or a matter of indifference, but also information and ideas that can

---

[227] Council of Europe, 'European Convention on Human Rights' 34, preprint 10.

[228] 'Guide on Article 10 of the European Convention on Human Rights' 11 <https://www.echr.coe.int/documents/guide_art_10_eng.pdf> accessed 17 August 2022.

offend, shock and disturb.²²⁹ The United Nations Special Rapporteur on Freedom of Expression has emphasized the same approach.²³⁰

Art. 10 of the ECHR is awarded a very wide scope, both in terms of the substance of the information and ideas that are expressed and the form that they might take.²³¹ This means that the Court's definition of what kinds of expressions is protected under art. 10 of the ECHR. Examples of forms of expressions that are included are:

- **Publications of photographs and photomontages:** In the case of ***Axel Springer AG v. Germany***, the Court ruled that fining a magazine and prohibiting further

---

²²⁹ 'Guide on Article 10 of the European Convention on Human Rights' (n 228) 11.

²³⁰ D McGoldrick, 'The Limits of Freedom of Expression on Facebook and Social Networking Sites: A UK Perspective' (2013) 13 Human Rights Law Review 125, 127.

²³¹ 'Guide on Article 10 of the European Convention on Human Rights' (n 228) 12.

publication of articles concerning the arrest of an actor for possessing cocaine.[232]

- **Artistic expressions:** In the case of ***Müller and Others v. Switzerland,*** the Court found that artistic expressions were within the scope of art. 10; *"Confirmation, if any were needed, that this interpretation is correct, is provided by the second sentence of paragraph 1 of Article 10 (art. 10-1), which refers to "broadcasting, television or cinema enterprises", media whose activities extend to the field of art. Confirmation that the concept of freedom of expression is such as to include artistic expression is also to be found in Article 19 § 2 of the International Covenant on Civil and Political Rights, which specifically includes within the right of freedom of expression information and ideas "in the form of art"."*[233]

---

[232] *Axel Springer Ag v Germany* [2012] ECtHR [GC] 39954/08.

[233] *Müller and Others v Switzerland* [1988] ECtHR 10737/84 [27].

These are examples of some of the types of expressions that are considered to be protected under art. 10 of the ECHR. Social media provides an array of different forms of expression, which also varies depending on what platform it is posted on. For example, on Instagram, the user-generated content is mainly image or video-based; within this, there can be both verbal and non-verbal expressions. On Twitter, there is generally considered to be based more on text-related forms of expression, whereas Facebook's user-generated content is a wide mix of forms of expression.

Art. 10(2) of the EHCR states; *"The exercise of these freedoms, since it carries with it duties and responsibilities, may be subject to such formalities, conditions, restrictions or penalties as are prescribed by law and are necessary in a democratic society, in the interests of national security, territorial integrity or public safety, for the prevention of disorder or crime, for the protection of health or morals, for the protection of the reputation or rights of others, for preventing the disclosure of information received in confidence, or for maintaining the authority and impartiality of* *the judiciary."*²³⁴ Just as the ICCPR the ECHR is not without limitations. When trying to determine whether interference is admissible, the Court analyzed whether it was; *"[...] "prescribed by law" and whether it "pursued one of the legitimate aims" within the meaning of Article 10 § 2, and lastly whether the interference was "necessary in a democratic society""*.²³⁵ This three-part test is very reminiscent of the test found in ICCPR.

In order for a limitation to be legal under art. 10, the interference has to be: ²³⁶

- **Lawfulness:** It is up to the national authorities and the national courts to interpret domestic law.²³⁷ Generally,

---

²³⁴ Council of Europe (n 227).

²³⁵ 'Guide on Article 10 of the European Convention on Human Rights' (n 228) 19.

²³⁶ 'Guide on Article 10 of the European Convention on Human Rights' (n 228) 19.

²³⁷ 'Guide on Article 10 of the European Convention on Human Rights' (n 228) 19.

the ECtHR is confined to looking at whether the effects of the interpretation are compatible with the ECHR unless there is a case where the interpretation is *"arbitrary or manifestly unreasonable."*[238]

- **Legitimacy:** Art. 10 holds the exhaustive list of what are considered to be legitimate aims of interference with the right to freedom of expression.[239] Those legitimate aims are found in art. 10(2):
  - National security
  - Territorial Integrity
  - Public Safety
  - Prevention of disorder or crime
  - Protection of health or morals
  - Protection of reputation or rights of others
  - Preventing the disclosure of information received in confidence

---

[238] 'Guide on Article 10 of the European Convention on Human Rights' (n 228) 19.

[239] 'Guide on Article 10 of the European Convention on Human Rights' (n 228) 22.

- o   Maintaining the authority and impartiality of the judiciary.
- **Necessary in a democratic society**: The Court has, through jurisprudence, developed the autonomous concept of: *"[...] whether an interference is "proportionate to the legitimate aim pursued", which is determined having regard to all the circumstances of the case using criteria established in the Court's case-law and with the assistance of various principles and interpretation tools."*[240]

For a limitation to the freedom of expression to be considered legal, it must live up to the three-part test found in the ECHR.

What is the application of the law?

Just as seen when looking at the application of the law in the chapter related to international law, this chapter will focus on the following:

---

[240] 'Guide on Article 10 of the European Convention on Human Rights' (n 228) 22.

- Exploring if the law can place obligations upon private actors directly or following the regulation would simply be a question of free will. This is interesting because it defines if adhering to the law can be seen as a choice or a matter of obligation for social media companies.
- Explore how regional law and institutions have regulated freedom of expression in specific situations and how the social media companies' guidelines and decisions might compare to this.

Who does the law apply to?

The ECHR places obligations upon Member States to not interfere with individuals' fundamental human rights, which is a negative obligation but also to protect individuals against human rights abuses committed by other private parties, which is a positive obligation. The ECHR does not place obligations upon private individuals or private institutions, such as the ones behind social media platforms directly, and the ECtHR cannot, as a rule, deal with complaints against them.[241]

There is no question that the ECHR protects the users of social media platforms from having their rights infringed by States. However, this raises the question of whether the ECHR can protect the users of social media platforms from having their rights infringed by the companies behind the platforms. As mentioned, the Court can only decide in cases where a State is involved. Therefore, they cannot decide in cases where there are solely private actors, such as in a case between a citizen and a private company. This type of case would have to be tried by national courts, who can decide in cases based on domestic law.

One way for a State to protect their citizens against having its rights violated by private actors, specifically true for social media, could be through ensuring effective remedies or implementing further national legislation either by implementing new legislation, or further develop existing legislation by editions or interpretation. This does, however,

---

[241] 'European Court of Human Rights - Questions And Answers' 5 <https://www.echr.coe.int/documents/questions_answers_eng.pdf> accessed 25 August 2022.

place the protection of individuals using social media and their right to freedom of expression outside the direct reach of the ECtHR and ECHR.

Through case law, the Court has explored State's positive obligations when protecting the exercise of the right to freedom of expression.[242] When the ECtHR places positive obligations upon States, this implies that; *"[...] the States are required to establish an effective mechanism for the protection of authors and journalists in order to create a favourable environment for participation in public debate of all those concerned, enabling them to express their opinions and ideas without fear, even if they run counter to those defended by the official authorities or by a significant part of public opinion, or even if they are irritating or shocking to the latter."*[243] This means that if the Court were to place positive obligations upon Member States, it would mean that the State would be obligated to ensure that

---

[242] 'Guide on Article 10 of the European Convention on Human Rights' (n 228) 12.

[243] 'Guide on Article 10 of the European Convention on Human Rights' (n 228) 12.

the freedom of expression of the individuals under their jurisdiction was sufficiently protected.

This notion of a positive obligation, in the case of freedom of expression under art. 10 of the ECHR holds the possibility for the ECtHR to exercise some control in cases between private actors. This is especially interesting when looking at cases where an individual might have had their right to freedom of expression limited by social media companies, through either their guidelines or through their enforcement of those guidelines.

The idea that a State has positive obligations is not new and has been imposed in different circumstances and under different articles. The Court has stated that there may be situations where the effective exercise of a fundamental right, not only depends on the States' duty not to interfere, but also on the steps they take to protect the sphere between private actors.[244]

---

[244] European Court of Human Rights, 'Research Report: Positive Obligations on Member States under Article 10 to Protect Journalists and Prevent Impunity' 10, 4.

The Court has established positive obligations in multiple cases, and in the case of **_Dink v. Turkey_**, the Court held; "*States had positive obligations in relation to freedom of expression: they must not just refrain from any interference but must sometimes take protective measures even in the sphere of the relations of individuals between themselves. They were also required to create a favourable environment for participation in public debate by all the persons concerned, enabling them to express their opinions and ideas without fear. In view of the authorities' failure to protect the journalist against the attack by members of an extreme nationalist group and his conviction in the absence of a pressing social need, the respondent State had not complied with its positive obligations with regard to the journalist's freedom of expression.*"[245] In this case the State had not lived up to its positive obligations and protected their citizen from having their right to freedom of expression violated by another private actor.

---

[245] ECtHR, 'Dink v. Turkey' <https://hudoc.echr.coe.int/eng#{%22itemid%22:[%22002-808%22]}> accessed 28 August 2022.

However, when establishing if positive obligations apply in a certain case, the Court will look at a number of factors. First of all, the positive obligation must not put an impossible or disproportionate burden upon States; it has to be something within the general reach of the State.[246] Secondly, the balance between the public interest and the interest of the individual has to be taken into consideration.[247] Thirdly, the scope of the obligation will not be the same in all cases, the individual State and their situation has to be taken into account, such as when it comes to priorities and resources, along with the difficulties when policing a modern society.[248]

When the Court has explored the idea of applying positive obligations under art. 10 of the ECHR would be possible; they have taken into account the kind of expression the case involves. This means that the Court must consider if the expression has the capability to contribute to public debates,

---

[246] European Court of Human Rights (n 244) 4.
[247] European Court of Human Rights (n 244) 4.
[248] European Court of Human Rights (n 244) 4.

the nature and the scope of the restrictions, the ability to use other venues, and if the right of others outweigh the right of the individual.[249]

Still, implementing positive obligations merely pushes States to seek to implement national measures to control interactions between private actors. This means the ECHR can only bind private actors indirectly, and if social media companies live up to the protection under art. 10 of the ECHR, it is a matter of choice.

How has the law been applied?

The ECtHR has, through jurisprudence, affirmed that art. 10 of the ECHR applies to the internet, and thereby also social media.[250] In fact, the ECtHR has stated that; *"[…] the internet*

---

[249] European Court of Human Rights (n 244) 5.
[250] Council of Europe, 'Freedom of Expression and Information' (*Freedom of Expression*) <https://www.coe.int/en/web/freedom-expression/freedom-of-expression-and-information-explanatory-memo> accessed 21 August 2022.

in it's very essence is comparable to other means of content delivery".[251] The Court has noted that user-generated content on the internet provides a unique platform on which to exercise the freedom of expression.[252] They state that the Internet plays an important role in the enhancement of the public's access to news and facilitating the distribution of information.[253] The Court has also stated that there is an increasing amount of information that is only available through the Internet, which means that there is an emergence of 'citizen journalism'.[254]

Though the Court has stated the positives of the emergence of the Internet, it also stated that there is a number of problems,

---

[251] RF Jørgensen, *Framing the Net: The Internet and Human Rights* (Edward Elgar Publishing Limited 2013) 55 <http://ebookcentral.proquest.com/lib/kbdk/detail.action?docID=1361996> accessed 21 August 2022.

[252] 'Guide on Article 10 of the European Convention on Human Rights' (n 228) 99.

[253] 'Guide on Article 10 of the European Convention on Human Rights' (n 228) 99.

[254] 'Guide on Article 10 of the European Convention on Human Rights' (n 228).

such as the fact that unlawful speech/harmful speech can be distributed widely in a short space of time;[255] *"It has acknowledged that the electronic network, serving billions of users worldwide, is not and potentially will never be subject to the same regulations and control, and that the policies governing reproduction of material from the printed media and the Internet may differ. The rules governing the latter undeniably have to be adjusted according to the technology's specific features in order to secure the protection and promotion of the rights and freedoms concerned."*[256] The Court also states that even though internet platforms such as social media, are powerful tools, the information that comes from them does not have the same *'synchronicity or impact'*[257] as broadcast information.[258]

---

[255] 'Guide on Article 10 of the European Convention on Human Rights' (n 228) 100.

[256] 'Guide on Article 10 of the European Convention on Human Rights' (n 228) 100.

[257] 'Guide on Article 10 of the European Convention on Human Rights' (n 228) 100.

[258] 'Guide on Article 10 of the European Convention on Human Rights' (n

Social media platforms actively censor user content daily, and sometimes there are valid reasons. Other times the reasoning behind the censorship might not live up to the standards outlined in the ECHR. This can both be true for too much censorship or too little. It is not generally disputed that there are limitations to the freedom of expression, but on the other hand, it is a central requirement for the existence of liberal democracy, and its further development that the freedom of expression is not limited indiscriminately.[259]

When looking at the cases where there is generally considered too little censorship, one usually thinks of 'hate speech'. Hate speech is a complicated matter, as there is a general consensus within the human rights community that it is a growing problem, carried along by the age of social media. However, there is no clear and undeniable baseline for what constitutes hate speech. In *Erbakan v. Turkey,* the Court stated that;

228) 100.

[259] Jacob Mchangama and Natalie Alkiviadou, 'Hate Speech and the European Court of Human Rights: Whatever Happened to the Right to Offend, Shock or Disturb?' (2021) 21 Human rights law review 1008, 33.

"[...]tolerance and respect for the equal dignity of all human beings constitute the foundations of a democratic, pluralistic society. That being so, as a matter of principle it may be considered necessary in certain democratic societies to sanction or even prevent all forms of expression which spread, incite, promote or justify hatred based on intolerance ..., provided that any 'formalities', 'conditions', 'restrictions' or 'penalties' imposed are proportionate to the legitimate aim pursued."[260] So, even if art. 10 of the ECHR protects forms of expressions that can be considered to be offensive, shocking and disturbing, it does not protect expressions that promote or justify hatred based on intolerance.[261]

When the ECtHR has examined cases with what can be described as hateful speech, the Court has generally taken two different approaches to solve the problem of limiting the freedom of expression:

---

[260] 'Fact Sheet - Hate Speech - European Court of Human Rights' 1 <https://www.echr.coe.int/documents/fs_hate_speech_eng.pdf> accessed 8 September 2022.

[261] 'Fact Sheet - Hate Speech - European Court of Human Rights' (n 260) 1.

- Exclusion from the protection of the Convention, under art. 17 of the ECHR, which prohibits the abuse of rights.[262] Art. 17 of the Convention states that; *"Nothing in this Convention may be interpreted as implying for any State, group or person any right to engage in any activity or perform any act aimed at the destruction of any of the rights and freedoms set forth herein or at their limitation to a greater extent than is provided for in the Convention."*[263] The Court has held that when it comes to cases of freedom of expression, art. 17 is only applicable in special cases; *"[...] only on an exceptional basis and in extreme cases, as indeed is illustrated by the Court's case law."*[264] However, it can be argued that this is not always the Court's approach, as they in **Norwood v. The United Kingdom** ruled that; *"The applicant's display of the poster in his window constituted an act within the meaning of Article 17,*

---

[262] 'Fact Sheet - Hate Speech - European Court of Human Rights' (n 260) 1.
[263] Council of Europe (n 227).
[264] Mchangama and Alkiviadou (n 259) 33.

which did not, therefore, enjoy the protection of Articles 10 or 14."²⁶⁵ Here the Court resorted to using the exclusion found in art. 17, without first looking to art. 10(2).

- Restriction to the protection of art. 10.²⁶⁶ These restrictions are found in art. 10(2) are, as previously mentioned; *"The exercise of these freedoms, since it carries with it duties and responsibilities, may be subject to such formalities, conditions, restrictions or penalties as are prescribed by law and are necessary in a democratic society, in the interests of national security, territorial integrity or public safety, for the prevention of disorder or crime, for the protection of health or morals, for the protection of the reputation or rights of others, for preventing the disclosure of information received in confidence, or for maintaining the authority and impartiality of the judiciary."*²⁶⁷

---

²⁶⁵ *Norwood v the United Kingdom (dec)* [2004] ECtHR 23131/03.
²⁶⁶ 'Fact Sheet - Hate Speech - European Court of Human Rights' (n 260) 1.
²⁶⁷ Council of Europe (n 227).

Herein lays the three-part test that has previously been discussed. The nature of hate speech is that it often, if not always, infringes upon the fundamental human rights of others, which can arguably create a strong basis for the lawful limitation of such speech under art. 10(2) of the ECHR.

The Court has had plenty of opportunity to rule in cases limiting freedom of expression. However, they have also had the opportunity to look at cases concerning limiting the freedom of expression online.

In **Delfi AS v. Estonia**, the Court decided on the liability of user-generated comments on an internet news portal. In this case, the applicant, the company Delfi AS, complained that it had been held liable by domestic courts for the comments posted on its internet page. In this case, the Court held that art. 10 of the ECHR had not been violated; *"It first noted the conflicting realities between the benefits of Internet, notably the unprecedented platform it provided for freedom of* *expression, and its dangers, namely the possibility of hate speech and speech inciting violence being disseminated worldwide in a matter of seconds and sometimes remaining remain persistently available online. The Court further observed that the unlawful nature of the comments in question was obviously based on the fact that the majority of the comments were, viewed on their face, tantamount to an incitement to hatred or to violence against the owner of the ferry company. Consequently, the case concerned the duties and responsibilities of Internet news portals, under Article 10 § 2 of the Convention, which provided on a commercial basis a platform for user-generated comments on previously published content and some users – whether identified or anonymous – engaged in clearly unlawful speech, which infringed the personality rights of others and amounted to hate speech and incitement to violence against them."*[268] In this case the ECtHR agreed with the ruling of the domestic court that the company behind the internet platform should be responsible for the

---

[268] 'Fact Sheet - Hate Speech - European Court of Human Rights' (n 260) 21.

content on their platforms, even if it is user-generated content. This case is interesting when looking at it in the light of social media platforms. This means that if the domestic courts had the opportunity to rule in similar cases against social media platforms, this would be in line with the ECHR and the ECtHR's interpretation of art. 10.

The case *Magyar Tartalomszolgáltatol Egyeülete and Index.hu Zrt v. Hungary* revolved around the liability of a 'self-regulatory body of internet content providers', and an internet news portal for comments posted on their websites.[269] The domestic court had ruled that the applicants were obligated to moderate the content of the user-generated comments on their platforms. Here the ECtHR held that art. 10 had been violated; *"It reiterated in particular that, although not publishers of comments in the traditional sense, Internet news portals had to, in principle, assume duties and responsibilities. However, the Court considered that the Hungarian courts,*

---

[269] 'Fact Sheet - Hate Speech - European Court of Human Rights' (n 260) 22.

when deciding on the notion of liability in the applicants' case, had not carried out a proper balancing exercise between the competing rights involved, namely between the applicants' right to freedom of expression and the real estate websites' right to respect for its commercial reputation."[270] Though the two cases can be argued to be very similar, in this case, the Court did not find the presence of hate speech; "*Although offensive and vulgar, the comments in the present case had not constituted clearly unlawful speech.*"[271] It is important to note, that even though the ECtHR use the term 'hate speech' in their case-law, there is no precise definition of the term, and there is currently no test or criteria set up for what constitutes hate speech.[272] It is the same for international human rights law, where, as previously mentioned, there is no general definition of hate speech. This means the ECtHR currently takes a case-

---

[270] 'Fact Sheet - Hate Speech - European Court of Human Rights' (n 260) 22.

[271] 'Fact Sheet - Hate Speech - European Court of Human Rights' (n 260) 22.

[272] Mchangama and Alkiviadou (n 259) 2.

by-case approach to defining what might fall within the definition of hate speech.

This case-by-case approach, with a lack of clear outlines of what defines hate speech, can make it harder for social media platforms, who would actively like to live up to regional human rights law, to figure out where the line is.[273] The Court has the opportunity to set up robust guidelines when to comes to regulating hate speech online, and those guidelines could be relied on by social media platforms.[274] However, it can be argued that the Court's current approach is not suited to the world of social media; *"On social media, context can change so easily since these are global platforms, whilst an online debate has no designated and well defined audience; the reader could be anyone. The Court's approach is not only irrelevant for such platforms but could constitute a dangerous template if relied upon by social media companies."*[275]

---

[273] Mchangama and Alkiviadou (n 259) 2.
[274] Mchangama and Alkiviadou (n 259) 34.
[275] Mchangama and Alkiviadou (n 259) 34.

As previously mentioned, social media platforms have extensive guidelines that, among other things, also touch upon the use of hate speech. However, social media platforms do seem to encounter many of the same problems as international institutions regarding hate speech, but without the strong set-up in legal institutions. Facebook has put up an article on its platform regarding hate speech. Here, they touch upon the difficulty in defining the term hate speech; *"People come to Facebook to share their experiences and opinions, and topics like gender, nationality, ethnicity and other personal characteristics are often a part of that discussion. People might disagree about the wisdom of a country's foreign policy or the morality of certain religious teachings, and we want them to be able to debate those issues on Facebook. But when does something cross the line into hate speech?"*[276] Here the social media company hones in on the problems that international, regional, and soft law encounters when limiting the freedom of

---

[276] Facebook, 'Hard Questions: Who Should Decide What Is Hate Speech in an Online Global Community?' (*Meta*, 27 June 2017) <https://about.fb.com/news/2017/06/hard-questions-hate-speech/> accessed 15 September 2022.

expression. When limiting expression online, how does one define what expressions are necessary to foster the right environment in a democratic society, and what expressions will undermine it? This is not a problem that only social media platforms face, but different from other environments, social media platforms work on a global scale, and that causes equally complex problems as the community is so diverse and the content is extensive. Facebook has stated that; *"Our current definition of hate speech is anything that directly attacks people based on what are known as their "protected characteristics" — race, ethnicity, national origin, religious affiliation, sexual orientation, sex, gender, gender identity, or serious disability or disease."*[277] This definition does reminisce of what has been established by the ECtHR. To name a few cases, there are:

- **Race**: In ***Glimmerveen and Hagenbeek v. the Netherlands***, the Court ruled that art. 17 of the ECHR did not permit the use of the freedom of expression

---

[277] Facebook, 'Hard Questions' (n 276).

under art. 10 of the ECHR to spread ideas that discriminate against race.²⁷⁸

- **Religion**: In ***Belkacem v. Belgium***, the Court decided that the applicant's expression about inciting violence against non-Muslims was in accordance with art. 17 of the ECHR, not protected under art. 10 of the ECHR.²⁷⁹

- **Ethnicity**: In ***Pavel Ivanov v. Russia***, the Court held that the anti-Semitic expression by the applicant was in accordance with art. 17 of the ECHR not protected by art. 10 of the ECHR.²⁸⁰

Twitter's definition of hate speech, or hateful conduct, is; *"You may not promote violence against, threaten, or harass other people on the basis of race, ethnicity, national origin, caste, sexual orientation, gender, gender identity, religious*

---

[278] 'Fact Sheet - Hate Speech - European Court of Human Rights' (n 260) 2.
[279] 'Fact Sheet - Hate Speech - European Court of Human Rights' (n 260) 3–4.
[280] 'Fact Sheet - Hate Speech - European Court of Human Rights' (n 260) 5.

affiliation, age, disability, or serious disease."[281] This once again mirrors what can be found when looking at the definition coined by Facebook, but it also somewhat mirrors what can be said to be the definition of the ECtHR. Also, the restriction of hate speech on the different social media platforms can be found in the community guidelines under the headline 'safety', meaning that content posted to the platforms may not pose a threat to other users. [282][283]

Arguably, this means that social media companies look to international- and regional human rights when they try to define and create limits on their platforms. This notion is also supported when looking at some of their cases. For example, one of the most high-profile cases of hateful speech on social media has been that of former President Donald Trump.

---

[281] Twitter, 'Twitter's Policy on Hateful Conduct | Twitter Help' <https://help.twitter.com/en/rules-and-policies/hateful-conduct-policy> accessed 9 October 2022.

[282] Facebook, 'Facebook Community Standards | Transparency Centre' (n 35).

[283] Twitter, 'The Twitter Rules' (n 65).

Following the insurrection at the U.S Capitol, Facebook decided to ban the Former President based on posts made in support of the people who engaged in the violent acts committed.[284] This decision was upheld by the Oversight Board, which was created to support Facebook when making decisions about freedom of expression on the platform.[285] The Board, which acts and an independent entity from Facebook, and is made up by various experts, stated that in the case of the Former President[286]; *"The Board upheld Facebook's decision, on 7 January 2021, to restrict then – President Donald Trump's access to posting content on his Facebook Page and Instagram account. However, it was not appropriate for Facebook to impose the indeterminate and standardless penalty of indefinite suspension."*[287] When deciding in this

---

[284] Oversight Board, 'Oversight Board | Independent Judgement. Transparency. Legitimacy - Decision FB-691QAMHJ' (n 145) Case decision 2021-001-FB-FBR.

[285] Oversight Board, 'Oversight Board | Independent Judgement. Transparency. Legitimacy - Decision FB-691QAMHJ' (n 145).

[286] Oversight Board, 'Oversight Board | Independent Judgement. Transparency. Legitimacy - Decision FB-691QAMHJ' (n 145).

case, the Board looked to the three-part test found in the ICCPR art. 19 (3). However, this test of lawfulness, legitimacy, and necessity/proportionality is very much reminiscent of the three-part test in the ECHR.

However, it is important to note that Facebook and the Oversight Board are not legal institutions, and do not have the same foundation to build upon when deciding cases of inadmissible content. They may be inspired by international- and regional human rights regulations, but this does not mean that the problem of lack of clarity and control of the outcome of the decisions made by the private actors has been solved. This has been illustrated multiple times both in cases where there has been a lack of consequence for hate speech, and where content has been removed from hate speech where there arguably was no talk of hate speech.

---

[287] Oversight Board, 'Oversight Board | Independent Judgement. Transparency. Legitimacy - Decision FB-691QAMHJ' (n 145) Case decision 2021-001-FB-FBR.

It is also important to keep in mind that the ECtHR has, in the last ten years, passed judgement in between 800-1600 cases yearly[288]. In addition, Facebook has stated that on a monthly average, they have deleted 288000 posts for hate speech alone.[289] This significantly higher number of decisions passed by Facebook will inevitably also result in more cases where the decisions might not be up to par with international law.

Sub-Conclusion

It can be concluded that art. 10 of the ECHR protects the right to freedom of expression online and offline. Just like the ICCPR, any limitations to the freedom of expression have the live up to the three-part test, whereby a limitation must be legal, legitimate, and necessary/proportionate in order to be considered legal under the ECHR. EHCR is legally binding for States, but it is not legally binding for private actors. However,

---

[288] 'The European Court of Human Rights In Facts And Figures 2021' 5 <https://www.echr.coe.int/Documents/Facts_Figures_2021_ENG.pdf> accessed 15 September 2022.

[289] Facebook, 'Hard Questions' (n 276).

the ECtHR places positive obligations upon States to make sure their citizens are able to enjoy their right to the freedom of expression. This is a way the ECtHR can try to influence States to regulate private actors, such as social media companies. Just like with the ICCPR, it can be considered quite problematic that there are no legal grounds for the ECtHR to regulate freedom of expression between private actors because compliance with regional human rights law is left to the free will of the companies. However, social media companies have recognized the ECHR as an inspiration they look to when deciding cases. This can be seen when examining statements, and also cases by the Oversight Board. The Oversight Board does not directly reference the ECHR, but due to the fact that they use the ICCPR and the three-part test as a guideline in their cases, which is incredibly similar to the test found in the ECHR, they also align with the ECHR.

Overall, it can be concluded that regional law, just as international law, has left the direct regulation of social media platforms largely outside their reach. This means it is a matter of choice if social media platforms align with regional regulation. However, in broad terms, it can be concluded that social media companies have acknowledged that they look to the ECHR when regulating content on their platforms.

In the following chapter, it will be summarized what the central problems are, which have arisen from the previous chapters. Furthermore, it will be explored what solutions there might be to the problems.

Assessment of policy

As explored in the previous chapters, international- and regional human rights law does leave something to be desired, regarding the protection of freedom of expression on social media. None of the laws that have been explored in the previous chapters have been able to place obligations directly upon private actors. This means social media platforms do not have to adhere to or align with international- or regional human rights law.

It can be argued that regulating global internet giants should be a job best left to international institutions that have the necessary heft behind them in the form of massive State support. On the other hand, it can be argued that neither international- nor regional instruments are meant to bind private actors; instead, they are meant to bind States. At the moment, the notion that States are the legal subjects of international- and regional human rights law is mostly winning out, at least when it comes to the instruments explored in this thesis. Therefore, there is reliance on States to regulate private actors or for private actors to regulate themselves.

It can be surmised that the direct regulation of freedom of expression on social media platforms has been left largely outside the scope of international- and regional human rights law. This means one must look to other solutions to solve the problem of this legal gray zone.

It can be concluded that though social media platforms might have an interest in aligning their guidelines, and decisions regarding the freedom of expression with international-and regional human rights law, they are not obligated to do so. This creates a precarious situation for users of the platforms, and for society in general because of the central role that social media plays in democratic debates. This begs the question of what can be done to create the necessary protection of the freedom of expression on social media platforms.

One way to solve the lack of reach of international- and regional law can be to develop regional law in a way where the instruments have a direct horizontal effect on private actors, and thereby afford better protection of the users of social media platforms. Another solution could be to look at the national level and develop national legislation. A third solution could be to continue to allow social media companies to self-regulate. These solutions are not all-encompassing, and there are other ways to solve the problem of lack of protection of the freedom of expression on social media, but these are the solutions that will be explored in the following.

Regional regulation

In the following, it will be explored how current regional human rights law could be utilized in a way where it would have a direct horizontal effect, and thereby bind private actors. Furthermore, it will be explored how new regional regulation might help to narrow the gray area, which has been left by current international- and regional human rights regulations.

Known regulation

The Charter of Fundamental Rights of the European Union (CFR) became legally binding upon the Member States of the

European Union when the Treaty of Lisbon entered into force in 2009, and was introduced as a way to bring consistency and clarity to the different types of human rights, found in both international law, regional law and among the Member States.[290] The CFR sets out not only civil and political rights but also economic and social rights.[291] The purpose of the CFR is that it brings together fundamental rights that can be found throughout different sources, both on an international- and regional level.[292] Art. 6 of the TEU provides that the CFR holds the same legal value as EU treaties and that it is legally binding.[293]

---

[290] Equality and Human Rights Commission, 'What Is the Charter of Fundamental Rights of the European Union? | Equality and Human Rights Commission' <https://www.equalityhumanrights.com/en/what-are-human-rights/how-are-your-rights-protected/what-charter-fundamental-rights-european-union> accessed 29 August 2022.

[291] Equality and Human Rights Commission (n 290).

[292] S Douglas-Scott, 'The European Union and Human Rights after the Treaty of Lisbon' (2011) 11 Human Rights Law Review 645, 651.

[293] Douglas-Scott (n 292) 651.

Art. 11 of the CFR protect the right to the freedom of expression.[294] The scope of the article corresponds to art. 10 of the ECHR.[295] Art. 11 of the CFR states that; *"1. Everyone has the right to freedom of expression. This right shall include freedom to hold opinions and to receive and impart information and ideas without interference by public authority and regardless of frontiers. 2. The freedom and pluralism of the media shall be respected."*[296] The provisions within the CFR are addressed to the EU institutions and bodies, and national authorities when they implement EU law.[297] Just like the ECtHR, the CJEU holds that the freedom of expression is

---

[294] European Union, 'Charter of Fundamental Rights of the European Union' 15, preprint 11.

[295] Agency for Fundamental Rights European Union, 'Article 11 - Freedom of Expression and Information' (*European Union Agency for Fundamental Rights*, 25 April 2015) <https://fra.europa.eu/en/eu-charter/article/11-freedom-expression-and-information> accessed 21 August 2022.

[296] European Union (n 295).

[297] European Commission, 'When Does the Charter Apply?' (*European Commission - European Commission*) <https://ec.europa.eu/info/aid-development-cooperation-fundamental-rights/your-rights-eu/eu-charter-fundamental-rights/when-does-charter-apply_en> accessed 25 August 2022.

one of the essential foundations of a 'pluralist, democratic society', which is one of the values that the Union has based itself on.[298]

The Commissioner for Justice, Didier Reynders has stated that; *"Our mission is to guarantee the protection of fundamental rights in our lives, no matter whether we interact online or offline. Fundamental rights ensure that we can be who we are; they enable us to participate in society in a meaningful manner. The Commission has made it a priority to shape the digital transition in a way that benefits everyone and leaves no one behind."*[299] The European Commission has made the digital transition, and the shaping of this initiative their priority to make sure it encompasses all.[300]

---

[298] Kellerbauer Manuel, Klamert Marcus, and Tomkin Jonathan, *The EU Treaties and the Charter of Fundamental Rights: A Commentary* (First edition, Oxford University Press 2019) 2133.

[299] European Commission, 'Protecting Fundamental Rights in the Digital Age' (*European Commission - European Commission*) <https://ec.europa.eu/commission/presscorner/detail/en/ip_21_6699> accessed 25 September 2022.

[300] European Commission, '2021 Annual Report on the Application of the

In the report from the Commission regarding protecting fundamental rights in a digital age, there is an emphasis on the fact that the offline world and the online world is hard to clearly distinguish from one another.[301] On the one hand, the Commission agrees that the digital age can help drive forth the fundamental rights by enabling individuals to make more use of rights such as the freedom of expression. However, at the same time, they also state that the technology also risks limiting the effect of the protection of human rights.[302] The Commission also recognizes that; *"Online intermediaries such as social media platforms play an important role in the life of every individual and foster new forms of interactions between individuals, public administrations and businesses. Their use has led to a significant increase in the information that is*

Charter of Fundamental Rights' (*European Commission - European Commission*) 7 <https://ec.europa.eu/info/files/2021-annual-report-application-charter-fundamental-rights_en> accessed 25 September 2022.

[301] European Commission, '2021 Annual Report on the Application of the Charter of Fundamental Rights' (n 300) 7.

[302] European Commission, '2021 Annual Report on the Application of the Charter of Fundamental Rights' (n 300) 7.

available to people and provides greater opportunities for people to exercise their right to freedom of expression and to access information, also creating multiple spaces for online activism and assembly of individuals and civil society."[303] The Commission has stated, following in line with the ICCPR and the ECHR, that content moderation must not be unnecessarily restricting, by ignoring the fact that freedom of expression still protects expressions that are considered to be critical, controversial, offensive or insulting to others.[304] This means that disinformation should not simply be banned, even though it might be offensive to others.[305]

It is important to note that not all forms of expression are protected; there are limitations. Just like the EHCR, the CFR does not protect forms of expression that deny events such as

---

[303] European Commission, '2021 Annual Report on the Application of the Charter of Fundamental Rights' (n 300) 8.

[304] European Commission, '2021 Annual Report on the Application of the Charter of Fundamental Rights' (n 300) 9.

[305] European Commission, '2021 Annual Report on the Application of the Charter of Fundamental Rights' (n 300) 9.

the Holocaust, as it may be considered an abuse of rights under art. 54 of the CFR.[306] Art. 52 (1) of the CFR holds the same three-part test of legality, which can be found in the CFR and the ICCPR.[307] This relates to art. 52(3) of the CFR, whereby; *"The limitations which may be imposed on it may therefore not exceed those provided for in Article 10(2) of the Convention, without prejudice to any restrictions which Community competition law may impose on Member States' right to introduce the licensing arrangements referred to in the third sentence of Article 10(1) of the ECHR."*[308] This means that interferences with the freedom of expression can be legitimate, if they comply with art. 52(1), and as a result of art. 52(3), and if they comply with art. 10(2) of the ECHR. Art. 52(3) of the CFR does not mention the case law from the ECtHR, but; *"[...] in J.McB. v L.E. the CJEU held in that where Charter rights are the same as those in the ECHR the Court of Justice should follow the clear and consistent jurisprudence of the*

---

[306] Kellerbauer Manuel, Klamert Marcus, and Tomkin Jonathan (n 298) 2133.

[307] European Union (n 294) preprint 52.

[308] European Union (n 295).

ECtHR."[309] This means that there is a strong link between the two legislations, and art. 52(3) aims to keep the link strong.[310] Any intervention must be 'necessary in a democratic society', and for art. 11 of the CFR, this means that there has to be a 'pressing social need'.[311] When it comes to the proportionality assessment, the important factors are, if the intervention has a 'chilling effect' on the exercise of the right to freedom of expression in the future, and if the expression is a matter of public interest. [312]

It is also worth noting that art. 53 of the CFR states that; *"Nothing in this Charter shall be interpreted as restricting or adversely affecting human rights and fundamental freedoms as recognised, in their respective fields of application, by Union law and international law and by international agreements to*

---

[309] Douglas-Scott (n 292) 655.

[310] Douglas-Scott (n 292) 655.

[311] Kellerbauer Manuel, Klamert Marcus, and Tomkin Jonathan (n 298) 2134.

[312] Kellerbauer Manuel, Klamert Marcus, and Tomkin Jonathan (n 298) 2134.

which the Union, the Community or all the Member States are party, including the European Convention for the Protection of Human Rights and Fundamental Freedoms, and by the Member States' constitutions."[313] This means that it is not only the ECHR that can serve as a minimum standard, but also international human rights instruments.[314] The CJEU is, therefore, able to take instruments such as the ICCPR into account when applying the CFR.[315]

The Commission has also stated that; *"The European Court of Human Rights has however also made clear that States are permitted and may even have a positive duty to counter all forms of expression that spread, incite, promote or justify hatred directed to persons or groups belonging to a particular ethnicity or religion."*[316] This means that the Commission also

---

[313] European Union (n 294).

[314] European Union Agency For Fundamental Rights, 'Handbook - Applying the Charter of Fundamental Rights of the European Union in Law and Policymaking at National Level. Guidance' 108, 25.

[315] European Union Agency For Fundamental Rights (n 314) 25.

[316] European Commission, '2021 Annual Report on the Application of the Charter of Fundamental Rights' (n 300) 9.

largely supports the stance of the ECtHR, when it comes to the positive obligations of the State.[317] They also state that though online platforms define their own guidelines, and thereby exercise their right to freedom of contract and right to do business without State interference, they should still seek to protect the rights of their users.[318] However, they do recognize that; *"There is not always a legal remedy available against such private decisions that would allow for such decisions to be balanced against individuals' rights and legitimate interests and ensure a certain degree of predictability. Where online platforms overly remove legal content, they may significantly restrict the freedom of expression and information."*[319] Their statement touches upon the core of the problem, which has also been seen when it comes to the reach of the ECHR and ICCPR. The protection of the individual against having their right to

---

[317] European Commission, '2021 Annual Report on the Application of the Charter of Fundamental Rights' (n 300) 9.

[318] European Commission, '2021 Annual Report on the Application of the Charter of Fundamental Rights' (n 300) 9.

[319] European Commission, '2021 Annual Report on the Application of the Charter of Fundamental Rights' (n 300) 9–10.

freedom of expression infringed upon by the private actors who own the social media platforms, is largely outside the direct reach of the regional- and international human rights courts and instruments. It can be argued that it is worrisome that regulation of large companies with an international reach is left to be governed by differing national legislation, if there even is national legislation.

Unlike the ICCPR and the ECHR, the CFR has the possibility of establishing a direct horizontal effect, which means that the regulation can become relevant in cases between private actors. This is interesting because this means that already existing legislation could place obligations upon private actors, such as social media platforms, if the scope of the use of direct horizontal effect were widened.

The CFR states in art. 51(1) that; *"The provisions of this Charter are addressed to the institutions and bodies of the Union with due regard for the principle of subsidiarity and to the Member States only when they are implementing Union law. They shall therefore respect the rights, observe the principles and promote the application thereof in accordance with their respective powers."*[320] However, this only referee to the binding effect upon public authorities, and establishes the vertical effect.[321] It does not expressively state its effect amongst private parties, which would establish a horizontal effect.[322]

The CFR encompasses both rights and principles, but a central requirement in the case law on the direct horizontal effect is that; *"[...] the provision concerned must be sufficient in itself to confer a right, no further elaboration or specification being necessary for its application."*[323] Even though it may seem like a straight forward requirement, it raises questions such as; *"the relevance of the reference to EU implementing measures*

---

[320] European Union (n 294).

[321] Nuria Bermejo, 'Fundamental Rights and Horizontal Direct Effect Under the Charter', *Fundamental Rights Challenges* (Springer International Publishing 2021) 11.

[322] Bermejo (n 321) 11.

[323] Sacha Prechal, 'Horizontal Direct Effect of the Charter of Fundamental Rights of the EU' (2020) 66 Revista de Derecho Comunitario Europeo 407, 18.

and/or national legislation or practices and, partly in the wake of that, the distinction between rights and principles, an issue far from clarified in the case law."[324]

In the case of **Werner Mangold v. Rüdiger Helm**, Mangold argued that national legislation, which allowed fixed-term-contracts for a maximum period of two years, and only longer if it was objectively justified, age discriminated because it did not provide protection for individuals over 52 years. [325] The Court stated that; *"It is the responsibility of the national court to guarantee the full effectiveness of the general principle of non-discrimination in respect of age, setting aside any provision of national law which may conflict with Community law, even where the period prescribed for transposition of that directive has not yet expired."*[326] The CJEU decided that national court should have set national legislation aside, which is contrary to the principles of non-discrimination, and where

---

[324] Prechal (n 323) 18.
[325] *Werner Mangold v Rüdiger Helm* [2005] ECJ Case C-144/04.
[326] *Werner Mangold v Rüdiger Helm* (n 325).

the rights afforded by the Charter is directly applicable the Charter can apply in cases between the private parties.[327]

The case of **Werner Mangold v. Rüdiger Helm** was regarding discrimination, but the Court has touched upon the idea that other rights might also be able to have a horizontal direct effect.[328] This can be seen in the case of **Association de mediation sociale v. Union locale des syndicats CGT and Others**, a case regarding national legislation violating art. 27 of the CFR, where the Court stated[329]; "*In this connection, the facts of the case may be distinguished from those which gave rise to Kücükdeveci in so far as the principle of non-discrimination on grounds of age at issue in that case, laid down in Article 21(1) of the Charter, is sufficient in itself to confer on individuals an individual right which they may invoke as such.*"[330] Currently, it seems like only a few of the

---

[327] European Union Agency For Fundamental Rights (n 314) 34.

[328] European Union Agency For Fundamental Rights (n 314) 35.

[329] *Association de médiation sociale v Union locale des syndicats CGT and Others* [2014] ECJ Case C-176/12.

[330] *Association de médiation sociale v Union locale des syndicats CGT and*

provisions of the CFR satisfy the requirements for implementing horizontal direct effect.[331] This means that it is up to the State to provide adequate protection of human rights between individuals through legislation, and/or enforcement authorities within the State.[332]

Unlike the ICCPR and the ECHR, the CFR opens to the idea of the direct horizontal impact, which can be seen in a multitude of other EU legislation, as well as the CFR. This direct horizontal impact could serve to bind the social media companies to already existing legislation, but it would mean that the current sphere of use would need to be widened to encompass art. 11 of the CFR.

New initiatives

As mentioned briefly, there is an option for the regional institutions to develop regional law further by implementing new legislation, in order to ensure it affords users of social

---

Others (n 329).
[331] Prechal (n 323) 18.
[332] Prechal (n 323) 18.

media platforms better protection. This would avoid, at least on a regional level, a patchwork of national legislation and self-regulation practices.[333] One such development is the Digital Service Act, which is the brainchild of the European Union.

In April 2022, a political agreement was reached on the Digital Service Act.[334] The DSA was formally adopted in July 2022 and will generally be directly applicable after fifteen months or from January 2024, whichever comes latest, after entry into force.[335] The DSA holds rules that aim to govern different

---

[333] 'At a Glance: Does the EU Digital Services Act Protect Freedom of Expression?' (*ARTICLE 19*) <https://www.article19.org/resources/does-the-digital-services-act-protect-freedom-of-expression/> accessed 3 October 2022.

[334] European Commission, 'The Digital Services Act Package | Shaping Europe's Digital Future' <https://digital-strategy.ec.europa.eu/en/policies/digital-services-act-package> accessed 3 October 2022.

[335] European Parliament, 'Digital Services: Landmark Rules Adopted for a Safer, Open Online Environment | News | European Parliament' (5 July 2022) <https://www.europarl.europa.eu/news/en/press-room/20220701IPR34364/digital-services-landmark-rules-adopted-for-a-safer-open-online-environment> accessed 4 October 2022.

services provided online, herein social media platforms.[336] It does not just aim to ensure the right to freedom of expression online, but it casts a much wider net.

The European Union has moved towards this notion by implementing the Digital Service Act (DSA), which aims to; *"[…] create a safer digital space where the fundamental rights of users are protected and to establish a level playing field for businesses."*[337] This piece of legislation seeks to consolidate already existing pieces of legislation, and self-regulation that seeks to regulate illegal or harmful content.[338] The DSA is not

---

[336] European Commission, 'The Digital Services Act: Ensuring a Safe and Accountable Online Environment' (*European Commission - European Commission*) <https://ec.europa.eu/info/strategy/priorities-2019-2024/europe-fit-digital-age/digital-services-act-ensuring-safe-and-accountable-online-environment_en> accessed 3 October 2022.
[337] European Commission, 'The Digital Services Act Package | Shaping Europe's Digital Future' (n 334).
[338] 'At a Glance: Does the EU Digital Services Act Protect Freedom of Expression?' (n 333).

a voluntary standard the EU Commission has the power to fine companies up to six percent of their worldwide turnover, if they do not comply with the rules.[339] For platforms such as Facebook, Instagram, and Twitter, this can result in fines that can amount to millions, and even billions of dollars.[340]

The DSA will be directly applicable across the EU, and some of the obligations found in the act are:[341]

- *"New measures to counter illegal content online and obligations for platforms to react quickly, while respecting fundamental rights, including the freedom of expression and data protection;"*[342]

---

[339] Reporters Committee, 'EU Poised to Impose Sweeping Social Media Regulation with Digital Services Act' (*The Reporters Committee for Freedom of the Press*, 9 May 2022) <https://www.rcfp.org/eu-dsa-social-media-regulation/> accessed 3 October 2022.

[340] Reporters Committee (n 339).

[341] European Commission, 'Questions and Answers: Digital Services Act' (*European Commission - European Commission*) <https://ec.europa.eu/commission/presscorner/detail/en/QANDA_20_2348> accessed 3 October 2022.

- *"Strengthened traceability and checks on traders in online marketplaces to ensure products and services are safe; including efforts to perform random checks on whether illegal content resurfaces;"[343]*
- *"Increased transparency and accountability of platforms, for example by providing clear information on content moderation or the use of algorithms for recommending content (so-called recommender systems); users will be able to challenge content moderation decisions;"[344]*
- *"Bans on misleading practices and certain types of targeted advertising, such as those targeting children and ads based on sensitive data. The so-called "dark patterns" and misleading practices aimed at manipulating users' choices will also be prohibited."[345]*

---

[342] European Parliament (n 335).

[343] European Parliament (n 335).

[344] European Parliament (n 335).

[345] European Parliament (n 335).

Furthermore, even stricter obligations have been placed upon online platforms and search engines that have 45 million users or more on a monthly basis, which will be enforced by the Commission.[346]

The European Commission President Ursula von der Leyen stated; *"Today's agreement on the Digital Services Act is historic, both in terms of speed and of substance. [...]It will ensure that the online environment remains a safe space, safeguarding freedom of expression and opportunities for digital businesses. It gives practical effect to the principle that what is illegal offline, should be illegal online. The greater the size, the greater the responsibilities of online platforms."*[347] Here, Ursula von der Leyen also directly addresses the notion of grading the responsibilities of companies by the size of monthly users. This is an interesting twist; it shows that the

---

[346] European Parliament (n 335).

[347] European Commission, 'DSA: Commission Welcomes Political Agreement' (*European Commission - European Commission*) <https://ec.europa.eu/commission/presscorner/detail/en/IP_22_2545> accessed 4 October 2022.

European Union believes there is a need to regulate internet giants such as Facebook differently from other online platforms.

The European Union has seen a need for new rules due to the development of digital services, and the way they have impacted the lives of individuals across the globe.[348] There is a general consensus that this development has brought many good things with it, but it has also brought new problems with it.[349] In the eyes of the European Union, these developments require a new updated legal framework that can ensure the safety of the internet users, and create a world where their fundamental rights are in the forefront.[350]

Only time will tell, if this new regional initiative will help to ensure the freedom of expression on social media platforms.

---

[348] European Commission, 'The Digital Services Act Package | Shaping Europe's Digital Future' (n 334).
[349] European Commission, 'The Digital Services Act Package | Shaping Europe's Digital Future' (n 334).
[350] European Commission, 'The Digital Services Act Package | Shaping Europe's Digital Future' (n 334).

On the one hand, an instrument on a regional level might help to avoid the patchwork of incompatible national legislation and also provide the opportunity to impose penalties upon the private actors who do not comply, which has arguably been lacking from previous legislation. At face value, the DSA provides the horizontal effect lacking in the ECHR. Since the DSA has yet to be seen in action, it can be hard to see if the instrument will have the desired effect and if the European Union will strike hard, using its newfound opportunity to enforce the rules upon the global internet giants.

National regulation

In the following, it will be explored how Germany has sought to adopt national legislation in order to regulate the gray area left by international-and regional law. It will also be explored how the United Kingdom is currently seeking to regulate the freedom of expression online in the future. Furthermore, there will be a focus on the positives and the negatives of this solution, to the lack of a binding legal framework to protect the right to freedom of expression on social media platforms.

Germany

Another solution is to compensate by implementing national legislation. This movement towards implementation of national legislation is already underway.[351] It has been seen in Germany with the Network Enforcement Act (NetzDG) from 2017, which sets up rules regarding the removal of 'illegal content'.[352] However, the NetzDG has been criticized for the fact that it violates the right to freedom of expression. The Human Rights Watch has stated; *"First, the law places the burden on companies that host third-party content to make difficult determinations of when user speech violates the law, under conditions that encourage suppression of arguably lawful*

---

[351] Jean Burgess, 'The "Digital Town Square"? What Does It Mean When Billionaires Own the Online Spaces Where We Gather?' (*The Conversation*) <http://theconversation.com/the-digital-town-square-what-does-it-mean-when-billionaires-own-the-online-spaces-where-we-gather-182047> accessed 3 October 2022.

[352] Human Rights Watch, 'Germany: Flawed Social Media Law' (*Human Rights Watch*, 14 February 2018) <https://www.hrw.org/news/2018/02/14/germany-flawed-social-media-law> accessed 4 October 2022.

speech. Even courts can find these determinations challenging, as they require a nuanced understanding of context, culture, and law. Faced with short review periods and the risk of steep fines, companies have little incentive to err on the side of free expression. Second, the law fails to provide either judicial oversight or a judicial remedy should a cautious corporate decision violate a person's right to speak or access information. In this way, the largest platforms for online expression become "no accountability" zones, where government pressure to censor evades judicial scrutiny."[353] This helps to illustrate how difficult it can be to implement national legislation that is supposed to regulate international companies. It is a difficult line for both companies and States to toe when trying to implement legislation that sets just enough boundaries, so hate speech does not make it onto the platforms, but also do not restrict the freedom of expression in a way where the fundamental right is compromised.

---

[353] Human Rights Watch (n 352).

The United Kingdom

Another example of national legislation in the making can be found in the United Kingdom. In terms of international law, the United Kingdom has ratified the ICCPR[354], and even though the UK has decided to leave the European Union, the country is still a participant to the ECHR.[355] For the United Kingdom, this means that they have to comply with both the ICCPR and the ECHR.

The United Kingdom has a system for prosecuting individuals using social media for sending or posting harmful content.[356] However, it is a system that relies on criminal prosecution of the individuals who produce the user-generated content, not

---

[354] Scottish Government, 'United Nations Treaties Ratified by the UK' <http://www.gov.scot/publications/united-nations-treaties-ratified-by-the-uk/> accessed 24 August 2022.

[355] Reiss Edwards-Amar Ali, 'European Convention on Human Rights (ECHR) Does It Still Apply After Brexit?' (*Lexology*, 12 April 2021) <https://www.lexology.com/library/detail.aspx?g=7e0577d5-e617-471a-8e00-5c964741965c> accessed 24 August 2022.

[356] McGoldrick (n 230) 131.

legal action against the social media platforms which has allowed the actions to take place on their platforms.

In the United Kingdom, the lack of due diligence from online platforms to tackle harmful content on their platforms has resulted in an increased interest in statutory regulation.[357] In 2018, a regulatory regime was proposed, which centered on 'statutory duty to care, to reduce online harm'.[358] The idea behind the regime was that it would regulate online services that live up to certain criteria's:

- Strong two-way or multiway communications component.[359]
- Displays user-generated content publicly or to a large group of people.[360]

---

[357] 'Regulating Online Harms - House of Commons' 9 <https://researchbriefings.files.parliament.uk/documents/CBP-8743/CBP-8743.pdf> accessed 24 August 2022.

[358] 'Regulating Online Harms - House of Commons' (n 357) 9.

[359] 'Regulating Online Harms - House of Commons' (n 357) 9.

[360] 'Regulating Online Harms - House of Commons' (n 357) 9.

This proposal was followed up by a polished version in 2019.[361] In this refined version, author Woods and Perrin, state that; "[...] *online environments reflect choices made by the people who create and manage them; those who make choices should be responsible for the reasonable foreseeable risks of those choices.*"[362] This means that the authors wish to hold the social media platforms accountable for the 'reasonable foreseeable risks' of the choices they have made when it comes to platform design and platform guidelines.

This resulted in a white paper that would look at the increasing liability of social media platforms for harmful and illegal content.[363] The 'Online Harms White Paper' claimed that; "[...] the existing "patchwork of regulation and voluntary initiatives" had not gone far or fast enough to keep UK users

---

[361] 'Internet Harm Reduction - An Updated Proposal by Professor Lorna Woods and William Perrin' 1 <https://d1ssu070pg2v9i.cloudfront.net/pex/carnegie_uk_trust/2019/01/27135118/Internet-Harm-Reduction-final.pdf> accessed 24 August 2022.

[362] 'Internet Harm Reduction - An Updated Proposal by Professor Lorna Woods and William Perrin' (n 361) 2.

[363] 'Regulating Online Harms - House of Commons' (n 357) 11.

safe. The White Paper therefore proposed a single regulatory framework to tackle a range of online harms.24 The core of this would be a new statutory duty of care for internet companies, including social media platforms. An independent regulator would oversee and enforce compliance with the duty."[364] The response to the white paper was mixed. The Open Rights Group held that social media platforms have played, and do play, a central role in protecting freedom of expression.[365] Furthermore, it stated that social media platforms play an especially important role for the freedom of expression of the youth.[366] In the opinion of the Open Rights Group, such regulations should be rooted in international human rights framework.[367] These opinions were shared by others. Damian Tambini stated that; *"[...] its proposals could be "significantly damaging for freedom of expression and pluralism". On the other hand, it could be "a proportionate and effective response" to internet harms."*[368]

---

[364] 'Regulating Online Harms - House of Commons' (n 357) 12.
[365] 'Regulating Online Harms - House of Commons' (n 357) 15.
[366] 'Regulating Online Harms - House of Commons' (n 357) 15.
[367] 'Regulating Online Harms - House of Commons' (n 357) 15.

In May 2021, a draft Online Safety Bill was published. The Bill's provisions; *"[...] would "put an end to harmful practices" online while protect freedom of expression and democratic debate."*[369] Just like with the Online Harms White Paper, the reaction to the draft of the Online Safety Bill has been varied.[370] One had, some argue that the draft Bill might limit the freedom of expressions, whereas others argue that it does not stretch far enough to protect individuals against harmful content.[371]

The Online Safety Bill has yet to be passed and is currently on hiatus until a new Prime minister has been found.[372] Some breathe a sigh of relief, where others lament the fact that the Bill has yet to enter into force. This shows how complicated regulating this gray area can be.

---

[368] 'Regulating Online Harms - House of Commons' (n 357) 15.
[369] 'Regulating Online Harms - House of Commons' (n 357) 28.
[370] 'Regulating Online Harms - House of Commons' (n 357) 33.
[371] 'Regulating Online Harms - House of Commons' (n 357) 33.
[372] Andre Rhoden-Paul and Kate Whannel, 'Online Safety Bill Put on Hold until New Prime Minister in Place' *BBC News* (13 July 2022) <https://www.bbc.com/news/uk-62158287> accessed 24 August 2022.

It is worth noting that even though international-, and regional instruments, and Courts, push States towards implementing national legislation to cover the area where international- and regional law is lacking. It is a difficult task for national law-markers to implement laws that regulate international companies that transcends borders. If States implement legislation that is too strict, companies might choose not to offer access to their platforms under those circumstances.

Social media companies constantly bud-heads with countries that impose strict rules upon them to either refrain from regulating freedom of expression, thereby allowing, for example, hate speech on their platforms, or restrict expression and thereby hinder the democratic process. One example of this is Twitter removing a tweet made by the President of Nigeria due to it breaching their guidelines for 'abusive behavior', and now Nigeria's government has decided to block access to the site for almost six months.[373] Another example is that both

---

[373] Eloise Barry, 'These Are the Countries Where Twitter and Facebook Are Banned' (*Time*) <https://time.com/6139988/countries-where-twitter-facebook-tiktok-banned/> accessed 3 October 2022.

Facebook and Twitter has been blocked in China since 2009, due to the platforms not conforming to China's restriction of censorship of non-governmental material.[374] Facebook and Twitter has also been banned in Iran since 2009, due to the fact that public government opposition thriving on the platforms.[375]

These are just a few examples of States that have decided to impose strict national legislation upon social media companies. Granted, these examples cannot be seen as situations where States wish to protect the freedom of expression on social media, but rather they want to limit it. Then again, future national legislation might have an interest in restricting some forms of expression on the platforms, with a legitimate aim, but this might prove to be too much censorship for the social media platforms. The companies might perceive it as a threat to the basis of their products. Mark Zuckerberg has stated; *"While our services, like WhatsApp, are used by protesters and activists everywhere due to strong encryption and privacy protections, on TikTok, the Chinese app growing quickly around the world,*

---

[374] Barry (n 373).
[375] Barry (n 373).

mentions of these protests are censored, even in the US. It's one of the reasons we don't operate Facebook, Instagram or our other services in China. I wanted our services in China because I believe in connecting the whole world and I thought we might help create a more open society."[376] This helps to illustrate that national regulation might create an impasse between States and companies. For some States, it is not seen as a loss, but if one looks at the statements of the United Nations Special Rapporteur, it is clear that access to online platforms such as social media must be a priority; *"[...] the Internet is one of the most powerful instruments of the 21st century for increasing transparency in the conduct of the powerful, access to information, and for facilitating active citizen participation in building democratic societies."*[377] This means that States when implementing national legislation

---

[376] Facebook, 'Mark Zuckerberg Stands for Voice and Free Expression' (n 18).

[377] United Nations, 'Promotion and Protection of All Human Rights, Civil, Political, Economic, Social and Cultural Rights, Including the Right to Development' (n 139) 4.

regarding freedom of expression on social media platforms must toe a difficult line.

As more and more States might decide to implement regulation, there will eventually be created a large patchwork of national legislation across the globe, which can make it nearly impossible for global social media companies to navigate. This patchwork of national legislation might not match one to one, or indeed be similar at all, as States might have different angles on their legislation and different interests they wish to cover. This may result in a very confusing legislative landscape, not only for companies but also the individual users of the platforms. Furthermore, when national legislation can end up creating a restrictive landscape it might even serve to undermine the idea of the freedom of expression being a universally applicable right that all individuals should be able to enjoy.

Self-regulation

Another way to tackle the gray zone left by international- and regional human rights law is by allowing social media companies to self-regulate.

Self-regulation can be defined as a company creating its own set of rules and guidelines, and then enforcing and upholding those without having external actors exercising control. There are several areas within the online human rights sphere, where regulation has been left ambiguous or has yet to catch up. The online sphere is constantly developing and more quickly than has been seen in other spheres. This means that parts of the online sphere, such as social media platforms, have arguably been left to their own devices while lawmakers have tried to catch up. As this thesis has previously explored, the direct regulation of freedom of expression on social media has largely been left outside the sphere of international- and regional human rights regulation. Soft law, such as the UNGPs,[378] have

---

[378] 'The UN Guiding Principles on Business And Human Rights - An Introduction' (n 125).

tried to help create a framework for companies to utilize, but as touched upon, these guidelines are not legally binding for companies. When international- and regional human rights law does not regulate freedom of expression online, self-regulation is an alternative.

Freedom of expression on social media platforms is becoming an increasingly popular topic among lawmakers on all levels of law, and more governments see a need for development in the legal foundation. Social media platforms have become the new 'town square', where people exchange ideas and express their opinions, which means that social media has become increasingly important for the democratic process.[379] Therefore, it could be worrisome if private companies were entirely in control of the regulation of content on their platforms, as they would be able to control much of the political debate.

It can be argued that due to the nature of the technology behind social media platforms, changes are happening too fast, and

---

[379] Burgess (n 351).

content reaches too far for governments to keep up. This is not a problem that is unique to the freedom of expression, but also when it comes to the right to privacy.

One way that international- and regional institutions can try to influence private companies to self-regulate is through instruments such as the UNGPs.[380] As touched upon, the UNGPs do not place legal obligations upon private actors, but they do try to set up a framework that companies might be able to look to when forming their guidelines, and options for remedies. However, it is a matter of choice for the companies whether they might choose to follow or implement the framework or not. Companies can also choose if they want to look to international- and regional human rights law, and case law to support and supply their own guidelines. It is completely within the rights of the companies, to make the determination not to follow the guidelines set forth by the United Nations. Arguably, this places users of the platforms in precarious situations. However, social media companies can have a keen

---

[380] 'The UN Guiding Principles on Business And Human Rights - An Introduction' (n 125).

interest in self-regulating, rather than having strict legislation imposed upon them. It gives them more room to maneuver, without having to worry about getting tangled in too much legislation. Mark Zuckerberg has stated that; *"We're increasingly seeing laws and regulations around the world that undermine free expression and people's human rights."*[381] This ties into the increase in national legislation, where some might not live up to the standards found in international or regional human rights law.

While clear rules and guidelines can be seen as a positive force for private companies, it can also be argued that large businesses can have an interest in keeping the legal gray zones, gray. When lawmakers start drafting legislation, the aim will often be to reach a democratic or moral high ground, but what is not usually factored into drafting legislation to protect human rights, is the economic aspect of maximizing earning potential. When companies self-regulate they are arguably in a

---

[381] Facebook, 'Mark Zuckerberg Stands for Voice and Free Expression' (n 18).

better position to protect their own interests, and those interests are often, if not always, to protect and increase their income.

Practicing self-regulation can be a challenge for platforms. In a case where the companies have an interest in keeping the area largely unregulated, they will also need to try to show lawmakers that there is no need to regulate a certain area. One way of doing this is by simply illustrating that the company's guidelines and internal regulation already are aligned with international- and regional regulations. So there is no need to establish formal obligations when the companies willingly will take on those obligations without having the element of force. It is not easy for companies to tread the line. For example, in 2016, Facebook removed an image of a girl, Kim Phuc, fleeing from a Napalm attack by a South Vietnamese Air Force Skyraider during the Vietnam War. The picture was taken in 1972, and by the photographer's admissions, the picture caused a stir when it was taken, and now it has caused a stir once again.[382] It is an iconic image, an image that has won a Pulitzer

---

[382] Mark Edward Harris, 'Photographer Who Took Iconic Vietnam Photo Looks Back, 40 Years After the War Ended | Vanity Fair'

Prize, and for most people, it is one of the photos that best describes the horrors of the Vietnam War.

When the photo was posted to Facebook, it was removed due to the fact that it did not comply with one of the guidelines, which is child nudity.[383] The photo was posted, among others, by Norwegian writer Tom Egeland.[384] Facebook has in their community guidelines stated that some content, which are against the guidelines might be allowed to stay on the platform, if it can be considered 'newsworthy' and it is in the 'public interest'. So why was the image removed?

<https://www.vanityfair.com/news/2015/04/vietnam-war-napalm-girl-photo-today> accessed 24 August 2022.
[383] Facebook, 'Facebook Community Standards | Transparency Centre' (n 35).
[384] Sam Levin, Julia Carrie Wong and Luke Harding, 'Facebook Backs down from "napalm Girl" Censorship and Reinstates Photo' *The Guardian* (9 September 2016) <https://www.theguardian.com/technology/2016/sep/09/facebook-reinstates-napalm-girl-photo> accessed 24 August 2022.

Facebook protected its decision to remove the content by saying; *"While we recognize that this photo is iconic, it's difficult to create a distinction between allowing a photograph of a nude child in one instance and not others."*[385] Here Facebook hits the nail on the head. It is difficult to distinguish from their guidelines alone, what content is allowed and what is not.

Facebook's policy rationale for why pictures containing child nudity are not allowed on the platform is reasonable. Here, they state that even when it is family who posts nude pictures of their children in good faith, they are removed to avoid the possibility of them being misused.[386] The arguments behind banning child nudity are reasonable. However, the point of the picture is not child nudity; it is about the powerful message it is supposed to convey, which should be encapsulated within the

---

[385] Levin, Wong and Harding (n 384).

[386] Meta, 'Child Sexual Exploitation, Abuse and Nudity | Transparency Centre' <https://transparency.fb.com/en-gb/policies/community-standards/child-sexual-exploitation-abuse-nudity/> accessed 24 August 2022.

exceptions to the guidelines Facebook has set forth. It is exactly on those grounds that Facebook has decided to allow the image back on the platform: *"Because of its status as an iconic image of historical importance, the value of permitting sharing outweighs the value of protecting the community by removal, so we have decided to reinstate the image on Facebook where we are aware it has been removed."*[387]

So, in this case, freedom of expression was reinstated, but it is a worrisome tendency. In this case, it was a well-known image, posted by an equally well-known individual with a platform with a wide reach, which meant that it was possible to create the necessary stir among users for the picture to be reinstated. Nevertheless, what about cases where these circumstances do not exist? Atrocities are committed every day all around the world. With platforms like Facebook acting as a new 'public sphere' where many people get their news, it is worrying that content that is newsworthy and in the public interest might be removed based on mistakes or differentiating opinions. This case also illustrates the indirect influence that users might have

---
[387] Levin, Wong and Harding (n 384).

on how companies might choose to regulate. Companies have an interest in controlling their image because image is a part of what they earn their profit on. As a general rule, no one wants to support a company with dubious morals, and users will actively unsubscribe when these dubious morals come to light.[388] A loss of users, and thereby a loss of profit, might push social media companies to self-regulate in order to save their image.

One way Facebook has tried to self-regulate is by implementing the Oversight Board, which has been mentioned throughout this assignment. Mark Zuckerberg has stated; *"I don't think we should be making so many important decisions about speech on our own either. We'd benefit from a more democratic process, clearer rules for the internet, and new institutions. [...] That's why we're establishing an independent Oversight Board for people to appeal our content decisions."*[389]

---

[388] Mary Meisenzahl Canales Katie, 'The 16 Biggest Scandals Mark Zuckerberg Faced over the Last Decade as He Became One of the World's Most Powerful People' (*Business Insider*) <https://www.businessinsider.com/mark-zuckerberg-scandals-last-decade-while-running-facebook-2019-12> accessed 5 October 2022.

The Oversight Board is still, arguably, a part of the Facebook regime, and cannot in good conscience be considered as an entirely independent means of remedy. It does, however, create a possibility of remedy by an organ that is not considered to be 'directly' under the control of Facebook.

Such initiatives as the Oversight Board might help to illustrate that companies, such as Meta, are aware that they hold an immense amount of power, and that this power should be checked. The point of the Oversight Board is that it is supposed to act as an independent instrument that is to review decisions made by Meta, but it does not take much to bring into question if this is the case. Due to the fact that the Board is funded by Meta, the members of the Oversight Board might not in all actuality enjoy complete autonomy when reviewing the cases.[390]

---

[389] Facebook, 'Mark Zuckerberg Stands for Voice and Free Expression' (n 18).

[390] Marta Maroni, 'Some Reflections on the Announced Facebook Oversight Board' (*Centre for Media Pluralism and Freedom*, 17 October 2019) <https://cmpf.eui.eu/some-reflections-on-the-announced-facebook-oversight-board/> accessed 5 October 2022.

Different from democratic institutions, those in power in private companies have not been elected through a democratic process. Instead, they can buy themselves said power, or they are paid directly by the company for doing their job. Therefore, they are going to have an interest in doing what is best for the company when it comes to economics. This also means that the interest in self-regulating in favor of protecting the right to freedom of expression might change over time, as Mark Zuckerberg has stated; *"[...] I'm not always going to be here, and I want to ensure the values of voice and free expression are enshrined deeply into how this company is governed."*[391] Generally, it is not in the best interest of the individual if the rights that they are afforded can change from one moment to another, based on the individuals sitting on the top of the pyramid. Arguably, laws are also influenced by the climate of those who have been elected. However, the law-making process is different from the process one can find within companies, where choices are very much driven by money and

---

[391] Facebook, 'Mark Zuckerberg Stands for Voice and Free Expression' (n 18).

the morals of the individuals who are in genuine control of the companies. Recently, one of the world's richest individuals, Elon Musk, has bought Twitter, intending to protect the freedom of expression on the platform.[392] On the one hand, one can argue that Elon Musk is acting in the best interest of the users of the platform. On the other hand, it is worrisome that one person can gain such power over a social media platform, and simply shift the way freedom of expression is regulated on the platform. This means that the guidelines can, in theory, change from day to day with no guarantee that it is for the better.

It is important to note that in this thesis, the social media platforms that have been chosen can be considered to be 'western' media, which is largely influenced by the western world. Another level of complexity can be added if the focus is turned toward social media platforms such as TikTok, which is based in China. It is no secret that China has a different political approach to freedom of expression than other countries, such as the United Kingdom; this might result in a

---

[392] Burgess (n 351).

baseline of freedom of expression, which might influence how and if the platform wants to align with international-and regional human rights law.

When it comes to self-regulating, it is worrying when individuals from within the companies step forth and argue that the companies are not necessarily interested in choosing morals above money. Whistleblower Frances Haugen, who was the former Facebook product manager, has stated; *"The thing I saw at Facebook over and over again was there were conflicts of interest between what was good for the public and what was good for Facebook. [...] And Facebook, over and over again, chose to optimize for its own interests, like making more money."*[393] This supports the idea that companies should not be completely left to their own devices because, in the end, the companies will choose to look after their own interests rather than protect the individuals using their platform.

---

[393] Press Association, 'Facebook Prioritises Own Interests over Public Good, Whistleblower Claims' (*TheJournal.ie*) <https://www.thejournal.ie/frances-haugen-facebook-messenger-profit-more-important-to-company-5564713-Oct2021/> accessed 2 October 2022.

Sub-Conclusion

It can be concluded that the protection of the freedom of expression is left largely outside the direct reach of international- and regional human rights law. This means that it is necessary to look at other solutions to ensure the protection of the freedom of expression on social media platforms.

The European Union Charter of Fundamental Rights has the potential to have a direct horizontal effect, which cannot be seen with the ECHR. This means that if the CJEU would widen the scope of application of direct horizontal effect, the art. 11 of the CFR which protects the freedom of expression, would be applicable in cases between private actors. This would be a way to bind private actors directly to an already existing legal framework.

Another solution on a regional level could be to implement new regulation which aims to regulate private actors, especially social media platforms. The European Union has recently been taking steps toward providing better protection of the right to freedom of expression online by implementing the Digital

Service Act. It is a framework that applies directly to social media companies and even seeks to regulate large platforms directly, and search engines with 45 million users or more a day, which is a new way to regulate the area. Furthermore, the European Union now has a way to enforce the new instrument, whereby any infringement can result in fines of up to six percent of their worldwide turnover. This new initiative, when it enters into force, might prove to be useful based on the fact that it can provide a streamlined instrument to the benefit of both companies and users. Additionally, the European Union now has an effective tool to ensure that the obligations within the Digital Service Acts are being upheld, and the consequence of not upholding those obligations are not inconsequential to the companies. However, if the instrument will prove to have the desired effect has yet to be seen.

Another option is to ensure that the right to freedom of expression on social media platforms protected is through national regulation. The movement towards implementing national regulation is already underway. Germany has already implemented the NetzDG to control the scope of freedom of expression online and draw it away from self-regulation by companies. The United Kingdom is implementing its own regulation. On the one hand, this means that there is a move toward States being more aware that social media companies are currently self-regulating, and trying to take over the gray zone in order to put forth clearer rules for companies to follow. On the other hand, if more States decide to follow in their footsteps, there will quickly be created a myriad of different legislations which will make it hard for the companies and the users to know what rules to follow and what rules they are protected by. Another point to note is that such a landscape might prove too much for social media companies to maneuver for one reason or another, and they might decide to draw back from the market. This would mean that the positive side of social media platforms, such as a higher engagement in the democratic process by individuals, will not be available.

It can be concluded that self-regulation is still a very large part of how freedom of expression is currently regulated on social media platforms. Therefore, a solution could be to keep allowing social media companies to self-regulate. There is an emergence of international guidelines, such as the UNGPs, to help and encourage companies to regulate in a way that is in line with international human rights law. It can be in the interest of social media companies to keep the area unregulated, to avoid having to navigate legal landscapes, and risk fines if they fail to live up to their obligations. This interest can also push companies in the right direction when self-regulating because if they do not move in the right direction, lawmakers might decide to step in. It is important to note that self-regulation carries a risk for the users of the platforms, due to the fact that the economic interest of the companies will arguably always win when the choice is between protecting fundamental rights and making money. Furthermore, the guidelines on social media platforms can change, almost from day to day, depending on who is 'in charge'. Therefore, it must be considered dangerous to allow the protection of the freedom of expression to fall into the hands of private actors instead of globally recognized and trusted legal institutions.

Conclusion

Social media platforms have enormous potential; for both good and bad. It has the power to affect people on a larger scale than ever seen before. Social media is a tool for modern-day expression that can spread information to a global network. It all depends on which ways it develops in the coming years. In order to influence this development for the better and to protect the freedom of expression, a central cornerstone in a democratic society, there is a need for a secure legal foundation so there is no a reliance on the goodwill of the companies behind the platforms.

The thesis explored how social media companies regulate their platforms. The platforms regulated the freedom of expression by implementing community guidelines and internal remedy measures.

Furthermore, the thesis analyzed the scope and application of the ICCPR, the UNGPs, and the EHCR. The thesis found that the ICCPR and the ECHR have largely the same scope and area of application. However, none of the regulations are legally binding for private actors. International and regional institutions can only influence private actors by two means. One is by pushing States to implement national measures, such as legislation or effective remedy options. Two is by imploring social media companies to align their measures with international- and regional human rights regulations, even though it is not legally binding for private actors.

It can be concluded through the analysis that social media companies seek to align with international- and regional human rights law. This can be seen in several different ways. Twitter, Facebook, and Instagram all stated that they lean on international- and regional human rights regulations when deciding how to treat the freedom of expression on their platforms. This is reflected in their community guidelines, and when examining their administrative actions on the platforms. A clear example of this can be seen when examining the Oversight Board, which uses the three-part test found in the ICCPR and ECHR as a standard for limitations Meta imposes have to live up to. The Oversight Board is also an example of Meta seeking to live up to the framework outlined in the

UNGPs. However, this system where companies choose to comply, instead of being bound to comply, leaves the users of social media platforms vulnerable. Without the safety of an enforceable, legally binding regulation that applies to social media companies, they freely decide that they no longer wish to comply with international- and regional human rights regulations.

Lastly, the thesis explored solutions to the problem having the regulation and upkeep of freedom of expression on social media, largely outside the reach of international- and regional human rights law, and mostly in the hands of the social media companies. One way would be, to further develop already existing regional regulations to have a direct horizontal effect and thereby be able to bind private actors. This would mean widening the scope of application of the CFR. However, there are signs that regional human rights law is moving towards implementing regulation that places obligations upon social media companies. The DSA is an example of how regional institutions are trying to develop regulation that aims to protect fundamental human rights, such as the right to freedom of expression, but is also equipped with the necessary penalty system. Imposing penalties is a strong vice; this would make it in the economic interest of the companies to comply in order to not receive massive fines for not protecting the freedom of expression on their platforms.

Another solution was implementing national regulation. This would be in line with how the legal landscape is currently shaped, where States regulate matters between private actors, and international and regional institutions mostly regulate States. However, it would also create a complex legal landscape for companies and citizens. Furthermore, it would be difficult for States to implement consequences for the lack of compliance due to the sheer size of the social media platforms.

The last solution that was explored was leaving companies to self-regulate. As of now, companies have done a fair bit to keep in line with international- and regional human rights regulations without being legally bound by them. It can be argued that they have a strong incentive to want to conform to international- and regional regulations. This incentive can be to curate the right image, so that users will stay on their platforms. The reasoning behind their choice to self-regulate can also be to show lawmakers that there is no need to implement laws, and thereby they can keep their legal flexibility. Though this incentive can be strong, and thus far, social media companies have complied without being legally bound to do so, it does not make for a strong foundation upon which human rights are sure to be protected. As long as there is no legal foundation that binds social media platforms, there will always be a reliance on companies' willingness to protect the freedom of expression on their platforms. It would be precarious for users of social media platforms if their right to the freedom of expression were to continue to rest solely in the hands of social media platforms, without the foundation of human rights regulation to lead them to the right path.

Overall, it can be concluded that social media protect freedom of expression on their platforms by implementing community guidelines, and then implementing consequences if said community guidelines are broken. Furthermore, all the platforms explored in this thesis have implemented internal remedy options, where decisions about removing content based on community guidelines can be reviewed. Meta has gone further and implemented the Oversight Board as an external review system to live up to the UNGPs framework of 'respect and protect'. Additionally, it can be concluded, by looking at the measures social media companies have implemented, that their measures cohere with the same protections arising under international and regional human rights law. However, it is not because international- and human rights law obligates them to cohere. As long as that is the case, the freedom of expression of social media users will be precarious.

Literature list

- Ali RE-A, **'European Convention on Human Rights (ECHR) Does It Still Apply After Brexit?'** (*Lexology*, 12 April 2021) <https://www.lexology.com/library/detail.aspx?g=7e0577d5-e617-471a-8e00-5c964741965c> accessed 24 August 2022
- Association P, **'Facebook Prioritises Own Interests over Public Good, Whistleblower Claims'** (*TheJournal.ie*) <https://www.thejournal.ie/frances-haugen-facebook-messenger-profit-more-important-to-company-5564713-Oct2021/> accessed 2 October 2022
- Aswad E, **'The Future of Freedom of Expression Online'** (2018) 17 Duke Law & Technology Review 26
- **'At a Glance: Does the EU Digital Services Act Protect Freedom of Expression?'** (*ARTICLE 19*) <https://www.article19.org/resources/does-the-digital-services-act-protect-freedom-of-expression/> accessed 3 October 2022
- Barry E, **'These Are the Countries Where Twitter and Facebook Are Banned'** (*Time*) <https://time.com/6139988/countries-where-twitter-facebook-tiktok-banned/> accessed 3 October 2022
- Baxi U, **'Market Fundamentalisms: Business Ethics at the Altar of Human Rights'** (2005) 5 Human rights law review 1
- Benesch S, **'But Facebook's Not a Country: How to Interpret Human Rights Law for Social Media Companies'** (*Yale Journal on*

Regulation) <https://www.yalejreg.com/bulletin/but-facebooks-not-a-country-how-to-interpret-human-rights-law-for-social-media-companies/> accessed 23 August 2022

- Bermejo N, **'Fundamental Rights and Horizontal Direct Effect Under the Charter'**, *Fundamental Rights Challenges* (Springer International Publishing 2021)
- Burgess J, **'The "Digital Town Square"? What Does It Mean When Billionaires Own the Online Spaces Where We Gather?'** (*The Conversation*) <http://theconversation.com/the-digital-town-square-what-does-it-mean-when-billionaires-own-the-online-spaces-where-we-gather-182047> accessed 3 October 2022
- Canales MM Katie, **'The 16 Biggest Scandals Mark Zuckerberg Faced over the Last Decade as He Became One of the World's Most Powerful People'** (*Business Insider*) <https://www.businessinsider.com/mark-zuckerberg-scandals-last-decade-while-running-facebook-2019-12> accessed 5 October 2022
- Council of Europe, **'European Convention on Human Rights'** 34
- Council of Europe, **'Freedom of Expression and Information'** (*Freedom of Expression*) <https://www.coe.int/en/web/freedom-expression/freedom-of-expression-and-information-explanatory-memo> accessed 21 August 2022
- Deplano Rossana and Tsagourias Nikolaos K, **'Research Methods in International Law: A Handbook'** (Edward Elgar Publishing 2021)

- Deva Surya and Bilchitz David, '**Human Rights Obligations of Business: Beyond the Corporate Responsibility to Respect'**? (University Press 2013)
- DigWatch, '**Freedom Of Expression Online In 2022 | DW Observatory**' <https://dig.watch/topics/freedom-expression> accessed 25 June 2022
- Douglas-Scott S, '**The European Union and Human Rights after the Treaty of Lisbon**' (2011) 11 Human Rights Law Review 645
- Dror-Shpoliansky D and Shany Y, '**It's the End of the (Offline) World as We Know It: From Human Rights to Digital Human Rights – A Proposed Typology**' (2021) 32 European Journal of International Law 1249
- Eberle EJ, '**The Methodology of Comparative Law**' 23
- ECtHR, '**Dink v. Turkey**' <https://hudoc.echr.coe.int/eng#{%22itemid%22:[%22002-808%22]}> accessed 28 August 2022
- Egan S, '**The Doctrinal Approach in International Human Rights Scholarship**' <https://papers.ssrn.com/abstract=3082194> accessed 6 October 2022
- Equality and Human Rights Commission, '**What Is the Charter of Fundamental Rights of the European Union? | Equality and Human Rights Commission**' <https://www.equalityhumanrights.com/en/what-are-human-

rights/how-are-your-rights-protected/what-charter-fundamental-rights-european-union> accessed 29 August 2022
- European Commission, **'2021 Annual Report on the Application of the Charter of Fundamental Rights'** <https://ec.europa.eu/info/files/2021-annual-report-application-charter-fundamental-rights_en> accessed 25 September 2022
- European Commission, **'DSA: Commission Welcomes Political Agreement'** <https://ec.europa.eu/commission/presscorner/detail/en/IP_22_2545> accessed 4 October 2022
- European Commission, **'Protecting Fundamental Rights in the Digital Age'** <https://ec.europa.eu/commission/presscorner/detail/en/ip_21_6699> accessed 25 September 2022
- European Commission, **'Questions and Answers: Digital Services Act'** <https://ec.europa.eu/commission/presscorner/detail/en/QANDA_20_2348> accessed 3 October 2022
- European Commission, **'The Digital Services Act: Ensuring a Safe and Accountable Online Environment'** <https://ec.europa.eu/info/strategy/priorities-2019-2024/europe-fit-digital-age/digital-services-act-ensuring-safe-and-accountable-online-environment_en> accessed 3 October 2022

- European Commission, **'The Digital Services Act Package | Shaping Europe's Digital Future'** <https://digital-strategy.ec.europa.eu/en/policies/digital-services-act-package> accessed 3 October 2022
- European Commission, **'When Does the Charter Apply?'** <https://ec.europa.eu/info/aid-development-cooperation-fundamental-rights/your-rights-eu/eu-charter-fundamental-rights/when-does-charter-apply_en> accessed 25 August 2022
- European Court of Human Rights, **'Research Report: Positive Obligations on Member States under Article 10 to Protect Journalists and Prevent Impunity'** 10
- Council of Europe, **'European Court of Human Rights - Questions And Answers'** <https://www.echr.coe.int/documents/questions_answers_eng.pdf> accessed 25 August 2022
- European Parliament, **'Digital Services: Landmark Rules Adopted for a Safer, Open Online Environment | News | European Parliament'** (5 July 2022) <https://www.europarl.europa.eu/news/en/press-room/20220701IPR34364/digital-services-landmark-rules-adopted-for-a-safer-open-online-environment> accessed 4 October 2022
- European Union, **'Charter of Fundamental Rights of the European Union'** 15

- European Union Agency for Fundamental Rights, **'Article 11 - Freedom of Expression and Information'** (25 April 2015) <https://fra.europa.eu/en/eu-charter/article/11-freedom-expression-and-information> accessed 21 August 2022
- European Union Agency For Fundamental Rights, **'Handbook - Applying the Charter of Fundamental Rights of the European Union in Law and Policymaking at National Level. Guidance'** 108
- Facebook, **'Hard Questions: Who Should Decide What Is Hate Speech in an Online Global Community?'** (*Meta*, 27 June 2017) <https://about.fb.com/news/2017/06/hard-questions-hate-speech/> accessed 15 September 2022
- Meta, **'Mark Zuckerberg Stands for Voice and Free Expression'** (*Meta*, 17 October 2019) <https://about.fb.com/news/2019/10/mark-zuckerberg-stands-for-voice-and-free-expression/> accessed 11 August 2022
- Meta, **'Facebook Community Standards | Transparency Centre'** <https://transparency.fb.com/en-gb/policies/community-standards/> accessed 11 August 2022
- ECtHR, **'Fact Sheet - Hate Speech - European Court of Human Rights'** <https://www.echr.coe.int/documents/fs_hate_speech_eng.pdf> accessed 8 September 2022
- Gammeltoft-Hansen T and others (eds), **'Introduction: Tracing the Roles of Soft Law in Human Rights'**, *Tracing the Roles of Soft Law*

in Human Rights (Oxford University Press 2016) <https://doi.org/10.1093/acprof:oso/9780198791409.003.0001> accessed 11 September 2022

- ECtHR, **'Guide on Article 10 of the European Convention on Human Rights'** <https://www.echr.coe.int/documents/guide_art_10_eng.pdf> accessed 17 August 2022

- United Nations, **'Guiding Principles on Business and Human Rights - Implementing the United Nations "Protect, Respect and Remedy" Framework'** <https://www.ohchr.org/sites/default/files/documents/publications/guidingprinciplesbusinesshr_en.pdf> accessed 12 September 2022

- Harris ME, **'Photographer Who Took Iconic Vietnam Photo Looks Back, 40 Years After the War Ended | Vanity Fair'** <https://www.vanityfair.com/news/2015/04/vietnam-war-napalm-girl-photo-today> accessed 24 August 2022

- Harrison N, **'Freedom of Expression in History and in Theory'**, *Circles of Censorship* (University Press 1996)

- Human Rights Watch, **'Germany: Flawed Social Media Law'** (*Human Rights Watch*, 14 February 2018) <https://www.hrw.org/news/2018/02/14/germany-flawed-social-media-law> accessed 4 October 2022

- Instragram, **'Community Guidelines | Instagram Help Centre'** <https://help.instagram.com/477434105621119?cms_id=477434105621119&published_only=true> accessed 11 August 2022
- International Justice Resource Center, **'European Court of Human Rights'** (10 July 2014) <https://ijrcenter.org/european-court-of-human-rights/> accessed 17 August 2022
- Carnegie UK Trust, **'Internet Harm Reduction - An Updated Proposal by Professor Lorna Woods and William Perrin'** <https://d1ssu070pg2v9i.cloudfront.net/pex/carnegie_uk_trust/2019/01/27135118/Internet-Harm-Reduction-final.pdf> accessed 24 August 2022
- Jørgensen R and Zuleta L, **'Private Governance of Freedom of Expression on Social Media Platforms'** (2020) 41 Nordicom Review 51
- Jørgensen RF, '**Framing the Net: The Internet and Human Rights**' (Edward Elgar Publishing Limited 2013) <http://ebookcentral.proquest.com/lib/kbdk/detail.action?docID=1361996> accessed 21 August 2022
- Jørgensen RF and Zuleta L, **'Private Governance of Freedom of Expression on Social Media Platforms: EU Content Regulation through the Lens of Human Rights Standards'** (2020) 41 Nordicom review 51
- Jørgensen RF and Zuleta L, **'Private Governance of Freedom of Expression on Social Media Platforms: EU Content Regulation**

through the Lens of Human Rights Standards' (2020) 41 Nordicom Review 51
- Joseph S, '**The Human Rights Responsibilities of Media and Social Media Businesses**' <https://papers.ssrn.com/abstract=3146730> accessed 30 September 2022
- Karen and Feldscher, '**How Social Media's Toxic Content Sends Teens into "a Dangerous Spiral"**' (*Harvard T.H Chan*, 8 October 2021) <https://www.hsph.harvard.edu/news/features/how-social-medias-toxic-content-sends-teens-into-a-dangerous-spiral/> accessed 16 August 2022
- Kellerbauer Manuel, Klamert Marcus, and Tomkin Jonathan, '**The EU Treaties and the Charter of Fundamental Rights: A Commentary**' (First edition, Oxford University Press 2019)
- Lagoutte Stéphanie, Gammeltoft-Hansen Thomas, and Cerone John, '**Tracing the Roles of Soft Law in Human Rights**' (First edition, University Press 2017)
- Levin S, Wong JC and Harding L, '**Facebook Backs down from "napalm Girl"** Censorship and Reinstates Photo' *The Guardian* (9 September 2016) <https://www.theguardian.com/technology/2016/sep/09/facebook-reinstates-napalm-girl-photo> accessed 24 August 2022
- Library DH, '**Research Guides: UN Human Rights Documentation: Universal Declaration of Human Rights**'

<https://research.un.org/en/docs/humanrights/undhr> accessed 17 August 2022

- Maroni M, **'Some Reflections on the Announced Facebook Oversight Board'** (*Centre for Media Pluralism and Freedom*, 17 October 2019) <https://cmpf.eui.eu/some-reflections-on-the-announced-facebook-oversight-board/> accessed 5 October 2022
- McGoldrick D, **'The Limits of Freedom of Expression on Facebook and Social Networking Sites: A UK Perspective'** (2013) 13 Human Rights Law Review 125
- Mchangama J and Alkiviadou N, **'Hate Speech and the European Court of Human Rights: Whatever Happened to the Right to Offend, Shock or Disturb?'** (2021) 21 Human rights law review 1008
- Meta, **'Child Sexual Exploitation, Abuse and Nudity | Transparency Centre'** <https://transparency.fb.com/en-gb/policies/community-standards/child-sexual-exploitation-abuse-nudity/> accessed 24 August 2022
- Meta, **'How to Appeal to the Oversight Board | Transparency Centre'** <https://transparency.fb.com/en-gb/oversight/appealing-to-oversight-board/> accessed 23 October 2022
- Meta, **'The Oversight Board | Transparency Center'** <https://transparency.fb.com/da-dk/oversight/> accessed 23 October 2022
- Miretski PP and Bachmann S-D, **'The UN "Norms on the Responsibility of Transnational Corporations and Other Business**

Enterprises with Regard to Human Rights": A Requiem' (2012) 17 Deakin Law Review 5

- United Nations, **'Hate Speech and Real Harm'** <https://www.un.org/en/hate-speech/understanding-hate-speech/hate-speech-and-real-harm> accessed 16 September 2022
- United Nations, **'Protect Human Rights'** <https://www.un.org/en/our-work/protect-human-rights> accessed 5 September 2022
- United Nations, **'The Foundation of International Human Rights Law'** <https://www.un.org/en/about-us/udhr/foundation-of-international-human-rights-law> accessed 17 August 2022
- United Nations, **'Universal Declaration of Human Rights'** <https://www.un.org/en/about-us/universal-declaration-of-human-rights> accessed 17 August 2022
- United Nations, **'What Is Hate Speech?'** <https://www.un.org/en/hate-speech/understanding-hate-speech/what-is-hate-speech?gclid=EAIaIQobChMIus6h2ruW-gIVh6jVCh0QzANSEAAYASAAEgINtfD_BwE> accessed 16 September 2022
- Ortiz - Ospina E, **'The Rise of Social Media'** (*Our World in Data*) <https://ourworldindata.org/rise-of-social-media> accessed 15 August 2022
- Oversight Board, **'Oversight Board | Independent Judgement. Transparency. Legitimacy - Decision FB-691QAMHJ'**

<https://www.oversightboard.com/decision/FB-691QAMHJ/> accessed 15 September 2022
- Oversight Board, **'Oversight Board | Independent Judgement. Transparency. Legitimacy. - Desicion 2022-006-FB-MR'** <https://www.oversightboard.com/decision/FB-E1154YLY/> accessed 24 October 2022
- Oversight Board, 'Oversight Board | Independent Judgement. Transparency. Legitimacy.- FB-JRQ1XP2M' <https://www.oversightboard.com/decision/FB-JRQ1XP2M/> accessed 17 September 2022
- Park S, **'The United Nations Human Rights Council's Resolution on Protection of Freedom of Expression on the Internet as a First Step in Protecting Human Rights Online'** 32
- Prechal S, **'Horizontal Direct Effect of the Charter of Fundamental Rights of the EU'** (2020) 66
- Rasche A and Waddock S, **'The UN Guiding Principles on Business and Human Rights: Implications for Corporate Social Responsibility Research'** (2021) 6 Business and Human Rights Journal 227
- House of Commons, **'Regulating Online Harms - House of Commons'** <https://researchbriefings.files.parliament.uk/documents/CBP-8743/CBP-8743.pdf> accessed 24 August 2022

- Reporters Committee, **'EU Poised to Impose Sweeping Social Media Regulation with Digital Services Act'** (*The Reporters Committee for Freedom of the Press*, 9 May 2022) <https://www.rcfp.org/eu-dsa-social-media-regulation/> accessed 3 October 2022
- Rhoden-Paul A and Whannel K, **'Online Safety Bill Put on Hold until New Prime Minister in Place'** *BBC News* (13 July 2022) <https://www.bbc.com/news/uk-62158287> accessed 24 August 2022
- Ruggie JG, **'The Social Construction of the UN Guiding Principles on Business & Human Rights'** <https://www.hks.harvard.edu/publications/social-construction-un-guiding-principles-business-human-rights> accessed 23 August 2022
- Sander B, **'Democratic Disruption in the Age of Social Media: Between Marketized and Structural Conceptions of Human Rights Law'** (2021) 32 European Journal of International Law 159
- Scottish Government, **'United Nations Treaties Ratified by the UK'** <http://www.gov.scot/publications/united-nations-treaties-ratified-by-the-uk/> accessed 24 August 2022
- Council of Europe, **'The European Court of Human Rights In Facts And Figures 2021'** <https://www.echr.coe.int/Documents/Facts_Figures_2021_ENG.pdf> accessed 15 September 2022
- Oversight Board, United Nations, **'The Oversight Board: Operationalizing the UN Guiding Principles on Business and

- Human Rights' <https://www.ohchr.org/sites/default/files/2022-03/Oversight-Board.pdf> accessed 23 October 2022
- United Nations, 'The UN Guiding Principles on Business And Human Rights - An Introduction' <https://www.ohchr.org/sites/default/files/Documents/Issues/Business/Intro_Guiding_PrinciplesBusinessHR.pdf> accessed 20 August 2022
- Twitter, 'The Twitter Rules: Safety, Privacy, Authenticity, and More' <https://help.twitter.com/en/rules-and-policies/twitter-rules> accessed 22 August 2022
- Twitter, 'Twitter's Enforcement Philosophy & Approach to Policy Development' <https://help.twitter.com/en/rules-and-policies/enforcement-philosophy> accessed 23 August 2022
- Twitter, 'Twitter's Free Speech and Rights of People | Twitter Help' <https://help.twitter.com/en/rules-and-policies/defending-and-respecting-our-users-voice> accessed 23 August 2022
- Twitter, 'Twitter's Policy on Hateful Conduct | Twitter Help' <https://help.twitter.com/en/rules-and-policies/hateful-conduct-policy> accessed 9 October 2022
- UNHRC, 'Faurisson v. France' (*Global Freedom of Expression*) <https://globalfreedomofexpression.columbia.edu/cases/faurisson-v-france/> accessed 16 September 2022
- UNHRC, 'Mukong v. Cameroon' (*Global Freedom of Expression*) <https://globalfreedomofexpression.columbia.edu/cases/mukong-v-cameroon/> accessed 16 September 2022

- United Nations, **'United Nations: International Covenant on Civil and Political Rights, CCPR/C/GC/34'** (1967) 61 American Journal of International Law 870
- United Nations, **'Hate Speech versus Freedom of Speech'** (*United Nations*) <https://www.un.org/en/hate-speech/understanding-hate-speech/hate-speech-versus-freedom-of-speech> accessed 16 September 2022
- United Nations, **'International Covenant on Civil and Political Rights'** (*OHCHR*) <https://www.ohchr.org/en/instruments-mechanisms/instruments/international-covenant-civil-and-political-rights> accessed 17 August 2022
- United Nations, **'International Human Rights Law -UN Actions against Hate Speech'** <https://www.un.org/en/hate-speech/united-nations-and-hate-speech/international-human-rights-law> accessed 17 September 2022
- United Nations, **'OHCHR | Instruments & Mechanisms'** (*OHCHR*) <https://www.ohchr.org/en/instruments-and-mechanisms> accessed 9 September 2022
- United Nations, **'OHCHR | International Human Rights Law'** (*OHCHR*) <https://www.ohchr.org/en/instruments-and-mechanisms/international-human-rights-law> accessed 10 September 2022
- United Nations, **'OHCHR Dashboard'** <https://indicators.ohchr.org/> accessed 17 August 2022

- American Civil Liberties Union, **'Promotion and Protection of All Human Rights, Civil, Political, Economic, Social and Cultural Rights, Including the Right to Development'** <https://primarysources.brillonline.com/browse/human-rights-documents-online/promotion-and-protection-of-all-human-rights-civil-political-economic-social-and-cultural-rights-including-the-right-to-development;hrdhrd99702016149> accessed 16 September 2022
- United Nations, **'United Nations, General Assembly, A/HRC/20/L.13'**
- United Nations, **'United Nations, General Assembly, A/HRC/38/35'** <https://documents-dds-ny.un.org/doc/UNDOC/GEN/G18/096/72/PDF/G1809672.pdf?OpenElement> accessed 15 September 2022
- Walker M and Matsa KE, **'News Consumption Across Social Media in 2021'** (*Pew Research Center's Journalism Project*, 20 September 2021) <https://www.pewresearch.org/journalism/2021/09/20/news-consumption-across-social-media-in-2021/> accessed 24 August 2022
- European Union, Grand Chamber, **'Association de médiation sociale v Union locale des syndicats CGT and Others'** [2014] ECJ Case C-176/12
- ECtHR, **'Axel Springer Ag v Germany '**[2012] ECtHR [GC] 39954/08
- ECtHR, **'Müller and Others v Switzerland '**[1988] ECtHR 10737/84

- ECtHR, **'Norwood v the United Kingdom (dec)'** [2004] ECtHR 23131/03
- European Union, Grand Chamber, **'Werner Mangold v Rüdiger Helm'** [2005] ECJ Case C-144/04

www.ingramcontent.com/pod-product-compliance
Lightning Source LLC
Chambersburg PA
CBHW050330220526
45465CB00012B/143